# Rural Reality

## Sixty Years of Family Farm Life

by

## Annette (Keppy) Remsburg

authorHOUSE™

*1663 LIBERTY DRIVE, SUITE 200*
*BLOOMINGTON, INDIANA 47403*
*(800) 839-8640*
*WWW.AUTHORHOUSE.COM*

*First published by AuthorHouse 10/20/04*

*ISBN: 1-4184-8827-5 (sc)*

*Printed in the United States of America*
*Bloomington, Indiana*

*This book is printed on acid-free paper.*

Excerpts from Daily Diaries
Written 1940-2000 —by
Myrtle (Eckermann) Keppy
*An Authorized Biography*

The primary source of information for this chronological narrative is the set of a dozen five year diaries kept by Myrtle. As she might say regarding well aged food in the fridge – these old diaries 'need using'. Coupled with biographical interpretation by their daughter, Myrtle and her husband Roy's 'rural reality' comes to life for the reader in a way that brings the past to the present for better viewing. We might begin to feel as if we can just call them up on their old wooden phone and exclaim (as she so often did), "Well...you're home!"

Roy and Myrtle Keppy with Alayna and Archie, May 2004

# Table of Contents

# Prologue

Who could have imagined the telling of this story could last more than sixty years? Daily diary entries are nearly uninterrupted! This book includes selected, but not edited, excerpts from those diaries. The story is told of the realities of rural living. Family farms of the latter half of the twentieth century were as dramatically affected by rapid changes as other parts of American society. Editorial text interspersed throughout explains some of the historical perspective as well as specifics of popular practices of the times.

It is not possible to know someone thoroughly. Without pretending to have captured the whole story, this history is based on real words written in real time, through more than six decades of family life. This writing represents a portrait of an American family of German ancestry. The ancestors settled in the Midwest to farm the rich land and raise quality livestock for food. Like a movie in full color, the drama moves through time and evolving life changes; farm girl and boy, young married farm couple in partnership, parents, grandparents, to wise sages with the perspective of having witnessed reality.

Myrtle's adventure in keeping a diary began when she received her first five year diary as a young girl for Christmas from her parents, Mildred and Valentine. After a late night out to celebrate the dawning of the new year—1936—Myrtle Adell Eckermann, age eleven, sat down in her bedroom after milking the cows on their small family farm to record the events of the day. This was to be the first of hundreds of days recorded in her beautiful handwriting in the first of more than a dozen of these precious little books.

Anyone who has kept a diary or journal knows how therapeutic the simple act of 'writing it down' can be, especially when life becomes a bit confusing. Myrtle did her best to include the relevant details of each day on the five short lines provided per day per year. Though primarily stating facts, an occasional feeling crept in. Roy carried on, with even more difficulty sticking to the allotted 5 lines, while Myrtle was hospitalized following several surgeries. Who would have guessed that he found this regular activity of hers so important and rewarding?

Descendents need a chance to 'get to know' these very special people. At this writing, 4 great grandchildren have been born to them (2 who currently live in Germany). It is for them, their siblings, cousins and all the in-laws and others interested in family farm life who may not know this history that the story of Myrtle and Roy Keppy is shared.

A genealogical search of family census records was not part of the scope of this biography. It is hoped that a family member may someday wish to obtain detailed information about this family's ancestry. Pertinent details known are included in this text and available at a glance in a timeline. As a primary source of historical documentation, Myrtle's diaries are invaluably saturated with situations of note to a genealogist: births, deaths, marriages. Yet even when noted on the day it happened, the past is so fluid that it is changed immediately, even in the memory of those who experienced it and wrote it down.

Whether written to put things in place or to pass on their traditions to future generations, diaries serve to acquaint family members with those who preceded them. This family has also contributed to the common good, and it is good to remember this.

"Pork People" who have known Myrtle and her husband Roy through the later half of the century will recall much of this tale. Active in the politics and promotion of the industry for many years, they left their mark for all to follow.

Supporters of numerous community interests, the Keppys even have a building at the Mississippi Valley Fairgrounds named in their honor. Though modestly noting that 'many others have done more', their record of involvement includes extensive participation and leadership in a variety of nurturing roles related to agricultural education through experiences offered to young people. This they sought for themselves when young and found they wanted to 'give back' through the years, as demonstrated in the following authorized biography.

Author's note: **Bold face type** has been used for all direct quotes from Myrtle's diaries. Entries are included as written with abbreviations, spelling and punctuation nuances. For example, the possessive apostrophe is not added when omitted. The reader will get used to the shortcuts. Of the more than 22,000 entries written by Myrtle through the years, some have been selected for inclusion in this biography for their commonality, others for their uniqueness. Explanatory editorial notes add insight as needed. Clarifying comments made by Myrtle and Roy during the time of this writing are an important aspect of the accurate portrayal of events, adding perspective and passion.

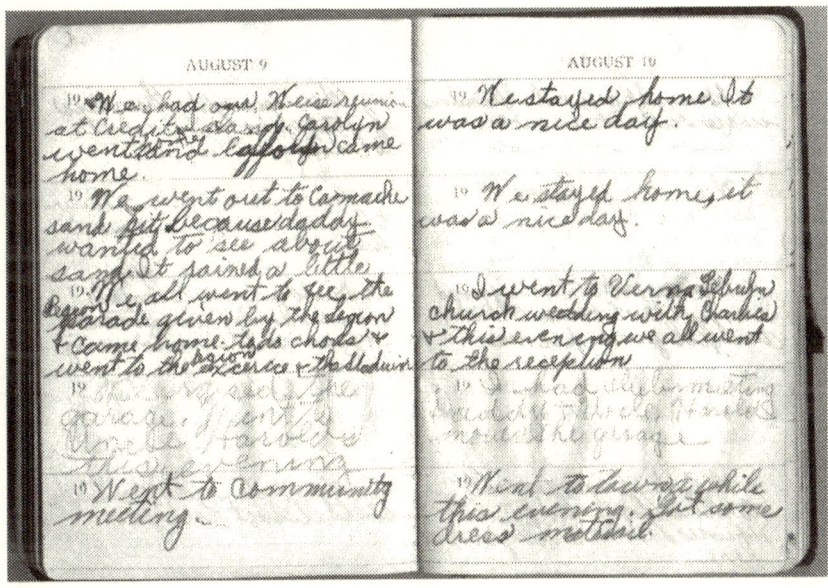

Scan of typical diary page

# Reverse Timeline

| | |
|---|---|
| 2004 | Myrtle and Roy celebrate the birth of two great grandchildren: Alayna 3/4 and Archie 2/7 |
| 2000 | Birth of first great grandson, Ethan 7/7 |
| 1998 | Birth of first great granddaughter, Baylee4/14 |
| 1996 | Birth of granddaughter, Hannah 3/9 |
| 1994 | Birth of grandson, Noah 6/3 |
| 1987 | Birth of grandson, Paul 3/13 |
| 1984 | Birth of grandson, Todd, 6/9 |
| 1988 | Death of Mildred (Weise) Eckermann 9/4 |
| 1981 | Birth of twin grandchildren, Kari and Kyle 8/6 |
| 1980 | Birth of granddaughter, Alysa 7/10 |
| 1978 | Birth of granddaughter, Shelley 10/3 |
| 1977 | Birth of twin grandsons, Neal and Chad 4/27 |
| 1973 | Birth of first granddaughter, Laurel 6/29 |
| 1970 | Birth of first grandson, Brent, 4/25 |
| 1965 | Death of Laura Wiese 4/21 |
| 1959 | Birth of daughter, Ila Jean, 3/24 |
| 1957 | Death of Anna (Danielson) Keppy 3/26 |
| 1956 | Birth/Death of daughter, Royce 10/19 |
| 1954 | Birth of daughter, Annette 2/5 |
| 1952 | Death of Valentine Eckermann, 1/31 |
| 1951 | Death of Henry Keppy Sr. 9/28 |
| 1949 | Birth of son, Dale 1/4 |
| 1947 | Birth of son, Glen 4/11 |
| 1946 | Marriage Myrtle Eckermann & Roy Keppy1/23 |
| 1935 | Death of Bertha Arp Steenbock |
| 1933 | Death of Jochim Steenbock |
| 1927 | Birth of Clifford Eckermann 9/16 |
| 1924 | Birth of Myrtle Adell Eckermann, 3/1 |
| 1923 | Birth of Roy Bert Keppy, 3/7 |

| 1899 | Birth of Mildred Wiese to Peter and Laura Steenbock Wiese 11/28 |
|------|------|
| 1899 | Marriage of Anna Danielsen & Henry Keppy 11/22 |
| 1885 | Anna (Danielsen) Keppy arrived in New York then by train to Davenport from Holstein, Germany |
| 1879 | Birth of Anna Danielson 9/21 |
| 1870 | Marriage of Bertha Arp and Jochim Steenbock 10/5 (Myrtle's great grandparents) |
| 1868 | Bertha Arp arrived in United States from Henstedt Holstein Germany |
| 1852 | Henry Keppy (Koeppe, Roy's grandfather) arrived in New Orleans then by Mississippi River to Davenport from Neustadt bei Magdeburg, Prussie (later called Germany) |
| 1849 | Birth of Bertha Arp (Steenbock) |

# Section 1

# Chapter One
# "The Home Fire"

*"The next thing most like living ones life over again
seems to be a
recollection of that life, and to make that recollection as
durable as possible
by putting it down in writing."*     Benjamin Franklin

Myrtle Eckermann's home as a child was not the
same house she left as an adult, though its location
was the same. All of her hard work put into polishing
woodwork, sewing curtains and ironing clothing went
up in smoke.

Myrtle learned the meaning of self-directed, regularly
scheduled hard work growing up on a farm. She sewed
most of her own clothes, cleaned every Saturday--
with special cleaning projects in between-- gardened,
canned and cooked. All this while, she attended school,
too! There was also time for some fun: riding their pony
Queen, going to movies, parties and plays. Following
are some prompted recollections of her childhood.

"When summer days were hot, (100 degrees plus)
we went swimming in the creek—it used to be pretty
deep. Or I would lay in front of the living room door.
There were such bad blizzards some winters that when
we went out coasting, we just walked right on top of the
hard packed drifts of snow—even right over the fence
tops!"

"We had a bath but no shower—running water but no
toilet, so somebody had to empty the pot from at night,

we just took turns. For a bath, we would sometimes heat water to put in the tub.

## 1940

**3/1 Got more little pigs today. Aunt Rubys and Grandpas were here for supper. Got saddle shoes, dress goods, anklets.**

Myrtle's sixteenth birthday is an example of how farm life is ever present, relatives are invited to share a meal for special occasions and simple gifts are cherished. Soon this family would have a rude reminder of just how precious home life can be.

Special entertainment was going to the theatre to see a movie. The Masquerade, a community party that participants went to masked, was a yearly event not to be missed. Favored also were birthday parties and bridal showers where one always came home with a unique handmade 'favor'.

In her second diary, the last page of memoranda notes, "To Myrtle for 1940 Christmas from Clifford." This space in the back of the little book also gave room for other gifts received as well as miscellaneous information such as the description of favors she made, "My colors were green to represent St. Patrick's Day. Had a ribbon drawn through a doily with a gum drop in it."

"When I was a little kid—about 8 or 9—we ate our first purchased bacon. We cooked it in a motel..." This might explain the fun she found in frying bacon in an electric skillet at motels through the years.

"My piano teacher came to our house to give me music lessons—that was the style then. I still feel guilty about not practicing the piano when my mother went out to do chores. When I heard 'Its high noon in New York and time for Kate Smith' on the radio, I just couldn't resist listening. She was such a wonderful singer", Myrtle notes apologetically. "I did get to sing in the Farm Bureau chorus with my neighbor."

Another main attraction was the annual fair. Farmers prize the soil itself as a major player in productivity and subsequent livestock nutrients. Competition amongst those growing crops is ongoing. Yields are measured and compared. Observation of neighboring farm fields occurs throughout the growing season. Finally, quality of the grain grown is assessed by experts at the annual County Fair. This was also a fine opportunity to get together with friends from across the county and have some fun. Myrtle says proudly, "My Dad was a really good farmer."

Women also competed at the fair with their canned goods, sewing projects and other homemaking efforts.

**8/14 Went to fair. Went home with Aunt Ruby's and came in to the grandstand at night.**

When President Roosevelt was inaugurated (see Presidents in Appendix), she notes, "My Dad liked him." What else does she remember about her parents? "They used a horse and buggy going to the Green Lantern Inn—a dance hall on Brady Street. Then they had a Model T.

Don't know how they ever got together. They would go to dances and, while waltzing, see people there." She remembers how much fun they had!

## Mildred, Clifford, Valentine and Myrtle Eckermann

Graduation from 'country school' in May 1938 prompted the purchase of a special dress. After 8th grade graduation, when many fellow students' formal education came to an abrupt end, Myrtle took entrance exams for high school and surprised herself by passing. She remembers signing up for high school 8/28/39 "had to take a big test...it was hard."

Eighth Grade Graduation

Some nights, or even weeks, she stayed 'in town' with Gumpa and Gumma Wiese and walked to school. More often, her father drove her. This gave them special time to visit. Though these conversations would most likely have been peppered liberally with German words and phrases, during the war years use of German in public was curtailed.

One of the many movies she attended, often with her little brother Clifford, was "The Grapes of Wrath", which she saw at the Uptown Theatre on Harrison Street March 10, 1940.

Clifford and Myrtle Eckermann circa 1938

The following day, while removing wallpaper and then burning it in the furnace, a spark ignited the roof and the house burned to the ground!

"We lost everything! The firemen even threw drawers out of upstairs windows, but almost everything was ruined. All we really had left was the clothes on our backs." Her diary was saved because it was in a kitchen drawer that was removed by the firemen. She and her younger brother and their parents lived in their garage from March 11 until June 6, when they moved down to the new cellar.

In a very untimely accident following the fire, "Daddy broke his arm...cranking the tractor."(3/15/40) The handle flew out at him. Nonetheless, March 17th "53 callers were here...to fix up wall." And again, on 3/22, "27 men for dinner...the neighbors helped!"

On blizzard days, the roads drifted closed. Groups of neighborhood men actually opened them with shovels! Each year in July, threshing oats and wheat was done together. The women prepared a picnic.

Myrtle remembers cooking on the wood-burning stove in the garage after their house burned down, feeding all the callers who were there to build a new house. Her worst memory of that spring was being cold all the time. The neighbors who came to help made all the difference in getting the family out of the cold garage and into the warmth of their new home. Her appreciation of such community caring may have prompted her selfless giving in time of other's need throughout her long life.

The new house that was built "...had everything— except a bathroom. My mother always kept the woodwork varnished. 'Saturday work' meant mopping on hands and knees, without sweeping first, and using the same bucket of water for the whole floor, including the stairs! I don't know why we had to do it that way or that often."

While mopping, she may have daydreamed about growing up to be useful in the world. What would she want to be? Country girls could either be teachers or office workers. In any case, she was thankful for the opportunity to go to high school. Later she notes that the most important thing she has learned in life is that, "You better get as much education as you can and learn how to get along with people."

"I had to wait a week to find out if I passed the test to get in. I was proud of my beautiful handwriting",

Myrtle remarks when recalling the test taken to enroll in Davenport Central High School.

Not surprisingly, her favorite classes were Home Economics and Bookkeeping, in which she excelled throughout her industrious life. As one of only a few students from 'the country', she experienced being in the minority. Sometimes she was called 'Myrt', which bothered her some. Some of her friends from high school remained friends for life. She enjoyed attending her Sixtieth class reunion.

Davenport High School graduation 1942

High School graduation was a proud moment, calling for a new dress and professional photograph. Shortly after the hoopla of graduation, Myrtle went to work in an office. She still – six decades later- lunches with 'the girls' that she met while working there.

During all these years, Myrtle became quite involved as a volunteer in the community, including 4-H and Rural Women's Institute.

**10/30 Went to Nat. Cornpicking today. I worked. Daddy was a gleaner. No school. Was a swell day.**

The National Cornhusking Contest was held in Scott County October 30, 1940. Myrtle helped sell concessions and her father was a gleaner, one who picked the ears missed by the contestants. Little did she know then that she would become much more familiar with the Keppy family farm where the contest was held.

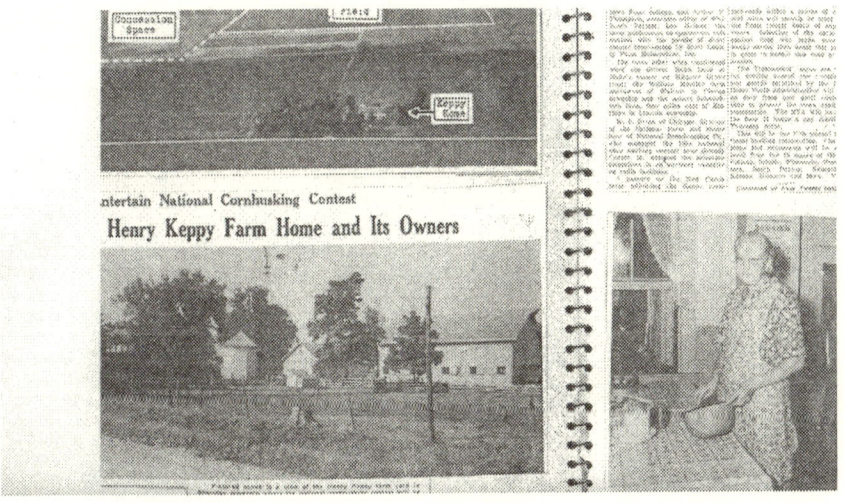

New Years eve seemed to entail an all-nighter, every year lasting a little longer than the last.

**12/31 Mamma and Daddy went to Walcott. Clifford & I stayed at Carolyns. We got home at 6. We milked & then slept all day.**

**1941**

**12/8 U.S. declared war on Japan at 3:00. Had the**

**school all together this morning to hear President Roosevelt talk to Congress.**

**12/13 Went to LeClaire Institute. I got 1ˢᵗ and 2ⁿᵈ on judging**. This was like a 4-H show. Early on, Myrtle learned to recognize quality and the correct way to do things.

**12/27 Short Course today. I was elected county president** (4-H) **I was presented with carnations from the county Club- gardenias. Dance eve.**

What kind of future was in store for this attractive young farm girl? Were marriage and a family to be part of her dream come true? How would she fulfill her mission in life?

# Chapter Two
# "Courted by Roy, the Boy on the Court"

*"Everyone's life is a fairy tale written by God's finger"*

Hans Christian Anderson

Myrtle feels she was in the right place at the right time (sort of like Cinderella?) when at a 4-H basketball game she met her new beau. Roy was the star of the champion team. She snagged him at the dance. Remembering meeting Roy at the game at Eldridge Turner Hall in 1942, my mother said, 'Those boys don't wear much clothes.' But they put on some clothes for the dance afterwards. He had to take Wilbur and Albert home (his cousins).

One of her best memories of high school; "I met Roy at the North door once in a while after school." When asked if she believes in love at first sight, she answers demurely, "Sometimes", and says she knew he was 'the one' "after sharing a few words". What advice does she have for young couples? "Do things together."

## 1942

**2/12 Went to basketball game this evening. Sheridan played Lincoln. Sheridan won by 7 points. There was a big crowd.**

**5/9 4-H girls took part in selling War Stamps from 9 to 9. I had to sell at Kinney's Shoe Store**

## 5/27 Met Roy's folks this evening and then went to Winfields roller skating party.

Tall, charming and very handsome, she didn't really expect to reel him in. They were both involved in township plays and found they could really do the 3-step dance together. Many shared 4-H events later, and visits to each others families while courting proved to reinforce their relationship. Their families were quite different. She the elder of two siblings, he the youngest of ten, their homes were worlds apart—though in neighboring townships.

The townships of Sheridan (his) and Lincoln (hers) are adjacent and centrally located in rural Scott County, Iowa. North and West of where the Mississippi River snakes along the east edge of the state, the farm land here is rich soil and flat enough that a person can see to the horizon. But it was a bit of a drive between the Eckermann and Keppy farmsteads.

One of the first times she was going to have dinner with his family, Myrtle was taken aback when she arrived at their home. She was appalled to see 2 big dogs on a chair in the kitchen! He defended their presence as hunting dogs, but she was not comfortable there all that evening. Her rule after marriage about no dogs in the house was breached when one was deathly afraid of thunder and firecrackers and came in under duress.

After Japan bombed Pearl Harbor and the U.S. entered World War II, curfews and rationing of gas, meat, cheese and fats began. Volunteer contributions of time and money were encouraged, and Myrtle did her best to help out through these difficult years, such as selling war stamps at a shoe store. She probably didn't mind this terribly, since shoe shopping was always of interest to her.

**6/8 Left DeWitt at 5am on the Chicago North Western**

"When my friend and I went to Chicago on the train, it felt like we were going to Europe", she says. "In those days you didn't go much. We took a weekend off and paid for the trip out of our paychecks." More fun followed.

**8/9 Work on my record book. Went for a motor boat ride—first one. Then went to see "Footlight Seranade".**

**9/6 Today Roy and I went to Muscatine to get watermelons. Ate in Wild Cat Den. This eve we rode the ferry over to Rock Island.**

Myrtle first worked outside the home at Triple A— Agriculture Adjustment Association—but when the war started and funding began to dry up, she was the first to be let go since she was the last one hired. "It was a blue day when the government funds were cut. She said, "A friend from high school who worked for International Harvester must have told them I was available because they called me. They really needed help then. But if a mistake was made I was blamed because I was a country girl."

**11/2 Got a raise today-.50 more. Now I get 3.25 a day.**

**11/29 Roy was over for duck dinner and then we went to Shrine Circus.**

**12/7 Worked today. One year of war. Went to Red Cross meeting tonight**

**12/25 Went to Grandpa's for dinner today. Roy was over this evening. I got a dresser set from him.** Myrtle showed the gift proudly in '03, "I still have it." The beautiful brush, comb and mirror sit on her dresser.

"When I was County 4-H President, my folks took me to Dewitt to catch the train to Ames. I think I bawled all the way! A taxi was to meet me. I stayed at Frylee Hall—such a big building! They didn't have a summer 4-H convention that year because of the war starting."

## 1943

**1/1 Slept from 5 this morning until 2 this afternoon. Then I made chicken dinner.**

**1/13 Roy was over for waffle supper. We put a puzzle almost together.**

**1/24 Went to Roy's sister for goose dinner. This evening we went to see 'For Me and My Gal". Sure was good.**

**1/31 Went to Roy's place for duck dinner. Played Monopoly and 500.**

**3/9 Roy was over this evening. I gave him my picture for his birthday.**

**3/27 Roy met me in town tonight. Had supper at the Times and then saw Lawrence Welk.**

**5/16 Went to Roy's place for the day. This evening we went to see "New Voyager".**

**12/24 Grandpa's were out. I got a cedar chest from Roy & 2 pair of hose, 2 scarfs, towels, dress & a slip.**

Considered to be a 'Hope' chest, the cedar chest may have been a rather presumptuous gift. Traditionally given to daughters by mothers in the days when girls brought dowries to a marriage, hope chests were to be filled with linens (often hand embroidered) and dreams of wedded bliss!

## 1944

**1/26 Went to Janice and George's wedding dance in Maysville. Had a swell time.**

**2/13 Stayed home all day. Was sorta cold. Got a valentine box of candy from Roy last night.**

Roy is really in the picture now! It seems like a lot of the diary entries have to do with eating together. Regarding the heart shaped Valentines candy, Myrtle said, "I've probably still got the box upstairs." (She did!)

**2/25 A transport plane fell in our back field about 4:30. The pilot was killed instantly. Pieces flew all over. Guard were here.**

She explained, "...the plane just came out of nowhere...it was kind of foggy. The pilot had brought a pair of silk stockings from overseas for his mother in Clinton, so he had gone out of the way...a diversion his commanding officer certainly would not have approved of, but his non-military mission was accomplished.

**2/29 Roy was here for steak supper. Later were in to see Ralph Hamman. Folks went to Eldridge.**

Her parents were often referred to as 'the folks' by Myrtle, but also Mommy and Daddy—even in later years.

Her great-grandparents were called Gumpa and Gumma (as in German) and her grandparents were either that or the more American titles of Grandpa and Grandpa. Roy called his 'folks' Ma and Pa and his grandparents the more traditional Grandpa and Grandma.

**3/1 Grandpas were here for supper. I had play practice. Daddy had elevator meeting. Got purse and gloves from Roy. A war bond, 2 slips, pajamas, blouse, hose, scarfs from the folks.**

**3/7 Roy got me from work tonight. Sure got to be bad weather out. Stay at Roy's place overnight and he took me to work.**

**4/15 Rained today. Went to see the captured German equip and then went to show and saw "Purple Heart"**

**5/7 Spent the afternoon at Roy's place. This evening we saw "Harvest Moon".**

**6/10 Got my driver's license this afternoon. This evening we saw Buffalo Bill".**

**6/20 Picked cherries tonight after supper & fell down with the ladder. Bought a war bond and got candy.**

**6/21 Picked cherries again tonight. Roy was over. He gave me an engagement ring. Later we went to show, "Weekend in Havana".**

**8/27 Went to Roy's family picnic.**

**12/7 I met Roy on the five o'clock Rocket** (train) **coming home from Chicago. He brought me pearls and hankies.**

These were the first of many thoughtful gifts he brought to her from his journeys. Though fancy cloth hankies soon came to be out of style as paper disposable tissues were made available, these gift hankies were most likely saved and cherished.

**12/24 Grandpas came out for supper. Roy was over and gave me blankets.** (Were these to be put in the cedar hope chest?) **I got a dress, slip, suitcase, billfold, ear rings, overalls, hose.**

Regular rural life in the forties carried its own set of simple pleasures and an acute awareness of family. Much cooperation was required in the endless daily hard work involved. The popularity of the President and the patriotism prompted by the war effort encouraged all to contribute to the best of their ability. The creed of 4-H lends itself to encouraging young people to participate: "I pledge my Head to clearer thinking, my Heart to greater loyalty, my Hands to larger service, and my Health to better living for my club, my community, my country, and my world."

*1945*

**1/4 Folks butchered two hogs today. Roy left for Cedar Rapids this morning to give his congress report.**(for 4-H)

**3/22 Bought a teal blue dress today.**

**4/12 President Roosevelt died this afternoon at 4:35 of a stroke. Truman is our new President.**

**4/26 Roy left for his physical at 6:15 this evening...**

**4/29 Roy came home from St Louis. He is 'limited service'. I went in at ten. Went to see Elnora** (Myrtle's sister-in-law who was married to Charlie and lived nearby on the original Keppy farm) **and the baby.**

Due to food shortages during the war years, many young farmers were exempt from service in the military. Roy was even more likely to be staying on the farm with his very flat feet. When he returned from his military physical with 'limited service' status, he and Myrtle were relieved but not surprised.

**7/22 Went to Ray's** (the youngest of Roy's 5 older brothers) **for picnic dinner. Roy cut and shocked oats. This evening we went to groceries picnic.**

To 'shock' grain means to gather and pile in shocks a number of sheaves (stems or stalks) stacked together on end to dry in the field.

Family picnics (or reunions) were annual events, of which Myrtle and Roy missed very few over the years.

**8/5 Went to Wiese family picnic. Roy didn't have to go home for chores so we saw "The Corn is Green".**

'Chores' were an every day part of life on the farm. It was quite a treat to be relieved of the pressing needs to feed and bed the animals—a little like going on vacation and letting someone else care for the pets—a necessary part of domesticating animals.

**8/2 Went to Roy's family picnic at Maysville today.**

**10/31 Stayed in from work and Roy came in and we had pheasant supper at his folks. (This was at**

the house where they moved to in town when retired from—or tired of—farming.)

**12/12 I took off from work this morn. Ma and I picked out my wedding dress at Neumans. Went to Aunt Ruby's** (Mildred's sister) **for supper for her birthday.**

**12/22 Cleaned today. Went to Nelda & Harveys wedding reception. Our wedding is in the Times tonight and the Sun Democrat.**

# Chapter Three
## *"It Was a Swell Day!"*

*Swell (slang) first rate; excellent: a generalized epithet of approval*

Webster's Dictionary 1991

Roy and Myrtle wed in Davenport, Iowa 1/23/46

**1946**

**1/11 ...last day of work—got a $100 check.**

**1/19 Cleaned the upstairs. This eve Ray's and Charlie's had a party for us. Got a set of dishes and a chamber.** (a pot to use at night instead of going to the outhouse)

**1/23 Our wedding day. There was a little sunshine, clouds, snow, and rain. Had reception and dance and supper. Had swell crowds.**

After being wed by a Presbyterian minister in a small church office on Perry Street in Davenport, Myrtle and Roy signed their marriage license. Along with their wedding party, ladies all in hats and gloves, the newlyweds joined family first at her home for cake and later were with friends for a lovely dinner and dance. They had already packed their bags for their honeymoon trip to Chicago.

**1/30 Went to the stockyards today and saw hog slaughtering and then to the Empire Room at the Palmer House.** (on their honeymoon)

What a dichotomy—from the kill floor to stately beauty! Was this to be the kind of life they would have together?

**2/4 We moved in our home today. Was a swell day. Also had dinner here.**

The Scott County, Iowa farm that Roy and Myrtle purchased was just around the corner from where he farmed as a boy. One of his older brothers, Henry

31

(known as Heiny), felt Roy should have that land and farmplace, so he and his wife helped out by loaning the down payment. The house was in very poor repair, its front porch sagging and shingle siding sliding out of place. Myrtle was not entirely thrilled with the house and yard. It had been left vacant, except for the unwelcome rodents. Roy said they would drive onto the yard and see hundreds of rats in their headlights! The voracious rats, which are unbelievably picky about their food being fresh, were fed precious ground beef with poison... and soon disappeared. She said it was just awful to give them that good meat, but worth it. Times were tough, and having fresh meat to eat was a treat, but ridding 'the place' of rats was of highest priority!

When commenting on the nice gifts he had given Myrtle before they were married and all the work done to the house they moved in to Roy said: "I always tried to keep Mom happy... Our place was such a mess—inside and out! I almost killed Grandpa Eckermann taking down a tree limb. We tied a rope to it and it was heavier than we thought...we learned a lesson."

**2/12...Had crow shooting here tonight. They got 59**. (Roy said, "Normal Meyer, brother-in-law, started that. They swarmed the pines.")

**2/18 The family and neighbors had a chevere on us tonight. About 80 were here...**(Myrtle clarified that it was a wedding surprise party, to which all brought sandwiches and cake to eat while playing cards)

Outbuildings included a big barn with a hay loft, a full sized corn crib, machine shed, hog barn and chicken coop, as well as an old milk house in the middle of the yard. The driveway was U-shaped and connected all of the buildings around the yard. There was a well and water pump, in addition to a 2-seater outhouse. Later, a cattle shed and 'new building' for hogs was added.

Several sections comprised the yard. A grassy area in front of the house was fenced down to the road. Several flower beds existed amongst the weeds. There were 3 raised round areas that some said were Indian burial mounds. Going through a gate around to the back yard led you to a large vegetable garden and more grassy areas. Behind the house and in front there were 2 huge Dutch Elm trees. Other shrubbery had gone wild and needed a lot of taming!

A big old chestnut tree stood sentinel beside the drive, truly a thing of outstanding natural beauty. J.R.Underwood (Extension Specialist extraordinaire) said the seed was probably brought from England, making the tree 100 years old when they moved in! Producing very large nut seeds, it was possible for them to plant more chestnut trees, but only one survived to thrive, even after its bark was scraped by a passing riding lawn mower driven by a sorry daughter.

The old chestnut tree in full bloom

As a landmark for the farm, the tree was a source of pride for the family as both grew.

The house itself was in very poor repair. Entering through the side door took you into the summer kitchen. This was only used when the weather got hot, providing a cooler venue for ambitious summer cooking and canning. To the left was the real kitchen, with stairs going up from it for the hired hand to have a private entrance to his room, which was later converted into the master bedroom after the extra stairs were removed. Through the large kitchen were stairs to the other part of the second story, where the family's 3 bedrooms were located.

Below those were 3 more rooms: the living room, the parlor, and the playroom/sewing room. The fancy parlor, with its grand bay window facing the front lawn and vast fields to the south, was separated from the living room by large wooden doors with glass knobs. The play room also had a door to close it off, as the bright west sun shone through the tall windows. Out the front door to the south off the living room was a porch with columns and cornices. Through a cellar luke outside, and later also via a door from the kitchen, was a dark and dingy laundry area and musty fruit cellar. Wrung out clothes and heavy wet sheets were carried in wicker baskets up out through the cellar luke to dry on the line in the steady Iowa wind. Though the wind often brought top soil and road dust, an electric dryer did not become an option until many years later.

The farm place was located on a dusty gravel road that ran East- West. Through the field to the South was the old one room country schoolhouse where Roy went to 9 grades, taught by his future sister in law, Jeanette. In the southeast corner of the farm was a tree under which was reportedly buried a young boy who died of scarlet fever. Beyond the north fields, there was a small creek and a 'pond' in the fields when it rained hard, which Roy's father taught him how to drain with tiles.

**4/1 I disked this afternoon while Roy went to Henry and put the hitch on.**

Myrtle noted that she really didn't do any field work 'at home'. Roy told of the day he had her do the disking because he had to go get the drill hitch on and he explained that she needed to overlap the rows. But while he was gone she thought she could get more done by not overlapping. So when he returned, the whole field was full of ridges and valleys and he had to do it over. He said, "That almost ended the marriage right then and there!" The look in his eye conveyed how emphatically he meant that!

**4/17 Was home all alone today. Worked upstairs all day. Dengler's were here & helped us with the chicken stove.**

**4/24 Went to Aaron's birthday party tonight. I cleaned the room above the kitchen & hung some curtains. No help today.**

This was unusual to be left alone with the work —people really pitched in to help get things done as needed! Myrtle and Roy helped in turn. There was great pride in really 'sprucing up' the farm. Myrtle was passionate about 'picking up the place', which meant getting rid of excess junk that may or may not be used in the future. She was always trying to 'get the weeds pulled in the fence lines'.

**8/11 We three pulled button weeds out of the bean field.**

Roy said that his dad asked "Are you going to get those weeds out of the beans"—so we did. The hired man, Frank, helped. The weeds were bad where we took down a building." he added.

**9/21 Went to Roy's mother's birthday this evening. I helped Roy pick corn this afternoon.** (She drove tractor pulling wagon while he picked by hand)

Myrtle said, "We milked 4 cows, churned our butter and gave skim milk to pigs. We raised ducks, too." That must have kept them busy! But it seemed that both had learned that hard work preceded head work in getting ahead in life.

**10/1 Mom was here this afternoon. We made butter.**

**12/26 Dressed five ducks today. Roy finished the linoleum laying.**

A wood fire would have to be built under the large copper pot for scalding feathers off of the butchered ducks (and chickens or geese). The water had to be kept boiling and the lid lifted only to dunk each fresh carcass. This same copper pot was used for washing clothes—first the sheets (with bleach) followed by the more soiled work clothes.

# Section 2

# Chapter Four
# "The Boys are Born"

*"In every conceivable manner, the family is link to our past, bridge to our future."* Alex Haley

**1947**

**1/1 Ray's and Charlies were here for 1:30 dinner**. ((So much for sleeping in—the men left for chores and came back to eat again)

**2/5 Roy's folks were out today & helped render out lard, grit sausage, swat sowa and cut the meat**.

Myrtle explained, "Swat sowa is pieces of pork put together (gel-like). We loved to eat it with fried potatoes. Another favorite part of butchering was grit vouse or blood sausage with syrup and fried eggs—made by stretching hog intestines, which had been boiled and soaked in salt water, over horns.

This sausage was made from fresh hog blood, which they would catch in a pail when a hog was butchered on the farm. Then it would be cooked down and added to barley, spices and raisins before being stuffed into hog intestines through a horn. It was usually served boiled with syrup and fried eggs. A little strange maybe, but absolutely delicious!

Grit vouse recipe or GRUTWIRST (minus the boiled blood and casings) :Soak in pork broth overnight; 2 lbs steel cut oats, 2 lbs. barley, 2 lbs raisins, 2T salt; add 1/2 t cinnamon, 1/4 t cloves; fry in lard cracklings (or butter) and simmer 20 minutes.

This was a favorite wintertime breakfast, because the hogs were necessarily butchered on a freezing day, and partially processed right on the farm. The pig was 'stuck', blood collected in a kettle, hair scraped from the skin, innards removed and discarded (except for the liver) head and feet cut off. Some people pickled the knuckles of the feet for a special treat and made 'head cheese' as well, with the original intent of preservation without the option of refrigeration. It was said that 'every part of the hog was used, except for the oink!'

**4/11 Glen Leroy was born at 12:43am. Roy stayed here until 6. Mom was in this afternoon. Roy was here both times. Room 414.**

Only recently have fathers been encouraged to participate in the birth of their children. At the time, he was treated as a visitor required to abide by two limited visiting hours per day.

**7/22 Glen turned over for the first time today. They started to combine wheat this afternoon.**

**8/13 Roy took his pigs** (to the fair) **this morning & then came out to get me. I was washing. Roy got a blue, red, 3 white & 1 pink.**(Blue being first place)

**10/29 I washed today. Went to Lawrence Welk tonight.** (Live!) **Roy got a record for singing the loudest**

**1948**

**3/23 ...joined Pythian Sisters...Elnora took me along. Roy delivered oats.**

**7/27 They didn't thresh today because of rain.** (Threshing—threw bundles in with pitchfork) **Went to town to Grandpa's and Roy's folks this eve to find hog book.**

**9/26 Went to Lake McBride with Martha's** (Roy's sister) **and Ralph's** (Roy's brother) **today. Roy sold 4 pigs to Ray and Charlie.**

That's seeing lots of family in one day! But that's what Myrtle loved to do.

**12/26 Roy went fox hunting awhile this morning & they got 1. Went over to folks for duck dinner.**

**12/27 Darlene was here today to get acquainted. Roy's folks were here awhile this afternoon. We dressed 25 chickens after lunch.**

**1949**

**1/3 Darlene started to work here this morning. She ironed. We went to town this afternoon. I to the doctor.**

**1/4 Dale Bert was born tonite at 6:55. Was a little sick all day. Just got to hospital on time. Sure was a foggy nite. Roy stayed till ten.**

**1/5 ...Roy gave me a dozen of roses.**

**1/7...got another bouquet of roses today to replace the other ones.**

Really quite a romanticist, Roy was not often noted as giving flowers, so this must have felt like quite a special occasion!

**1/10 Came home today. My 6ᵗʰ day. Darlene washed. Glen loves the baby. Dale woke at 12:30 & 4 and 8. Grandpas were out.**

**1/11 Darlene had to quit today as they were moving.**

**8/17 Went to the fair today. Roy won $165.00 of prize money. Had boys along.**

With the birth of their first child, Myrtle found herself more bound to the house. This became even more true with the birth of their second son two years later, Before long, 'the boys' were most often tagging along with their dad, helping with the livestock chores and riding on the fender of the tractor for hours , watching and learning as the field work was done. Soon enough they were actually able to help, spending all of their time outside when not in school or at sports practices.

### 1950

**1/11 Roy donated blood to the blood bank this noon. Was in by the folks all day.** Donating with 'the someone else will need it' spirit, Roy was thankful later in life to those who give blood as repeated transfusions helped him to survive the ravages of leukemia.

**1/14 Did my cleaning. All took baths tonite. Was terrible windy.**

**1/18 Roy and I made grit vouse & after lunch we went to town awhile & had meat ground. Went to basketball game with Walt and Elaine.**

**2/19 On our way home from town about 4:30 Glen fell from car. Took him to Mercy. Had stitches taken. Both boys sitting in back. Was terrible.**

Very few signs of emotion are entered into the limited space of the diaries; the most powerful being expressed in a matter-of-fact way (i.e.: was terrible, when Glen fell) Car seats for infants and young children had not yet been invented; nor had seat belts, for that matter. A push down door lock could easily be pulled up to unlock the door. No one had heard of child-safety locks, which were surely developed due to just this sort of 'terrible' accident.

**3/25 Went to hog show about 10. Took Glen along and Dale stayed at Roy's Mom. Roy got 11th and 19th.**

**7/4 Had Keppy picnic here today. Went to Walt's this eve to watch fireworks.**

**7/19 Rained almost all day. Roy made out pedigree papers and I mended.**

In order to raise purebred hogs, careful records were kept. Crossbreeding called for even more complicated paperwork.

In retrospect, Myrtle sites her favorite year as when she married. The highlight of her life was her children. In the words of Weathorford,

*"The value of a life is best measured by moments spent giving one's self...sharing wisdom, inspiring hope, wiping tears and touching hearts."*

# Chapter Five
# "The Family Grows on the Growing Farm"

*"Naturally, Young people eventually determine their own values. But all of us have an obligation at least to expose them to our own experience, learning, and aspirations."*

--David Rockefeller

Just as a hummingbird floats gently and quickly from flower to flower drinking in the life sustaining nectar, Myrtle and Roy tackled each of the unending tasks of homemaking and farming with determination and confidence. There were fields to be plowed, hogs to be housed, and tomatoes to be canned. Walls needed washing and wallpaper had to be replaced. Stinky work clothes needed to be laundered in the cellar and clucking chickens needed to be butchered on the stump, then dressed in the summer kitchen. Modern technologies beyond the roller wringer and iron were not even in her repertoire of dreams, much less flash-frozen chicken breasts at the ready for a quick meal.

Myrtle often said, "I'm not happy unless I'm busy." A woman in constant motion, she felt the need to fill the day with useful activity, as reflected in her diaries. She spent hours in her kitchen..."I liked to cook—"the more the merrier"—of course when cooking for many, she said she didn't always like it, though she found satisfaction in 'seeing the men fed'. What she really didn't like was when the men didn't come in on time—which was almost always. She said Grandma Keppy (Roy's mother) had a solution for that; hitting the porch door was their signal that it was time to eat.

'Dinner' on the farm was the noon meal, with 'lunch' referring to mid-morning or mid-afternoon snacks. 'Supper' was a simpler meal often served after dark.

Myrtle's role as supporter and sustainer was surely more complicated than that of her city counterparts. On the farm, the rhythms of the workload based on planting and harvesting also dictated Myrtle's workday. She may be called upon to 'run for parts' if machinery broke down just before a meal was to be served. Or a sudden rain shower may send the men in early for their noon dinner.

The keeper of the castle might be found in the cellar laundering with lethal lye soap smells giving away her location. Her great escape on those days was to carry the wicker baskets full of steaming hot and heavy wet clothes out to hang in the automatic dryer consisting of dusty prairie winds.

Another favorite hide out of hers was the vegetable garden behind the house. In early spring the soil needed preparation and planting. Thereafter, plants needed more attention than could be given throughout the busy summer and fall. Canning days were never cool, but she carried out this hot task as needed to store the abundance of garden produce. Use of the freezer for this purpose became more common in later years.

Myrtle was a marvelous helpmate, doing all the cooking (even for the hired help), laundry (which was often not a pretty sight when dumped dirty in the cellar), endless cleaning as well as the bookkeeping. She also shoveled manure or drove tractor as needed. Never an idle moment! Her vision of the place—with all the junk piles cleaned up—and her insights into management complemented Roy's. That is not to say they never disagreed. But, in the end, they proceeded like a team of well trained work horses, harnessed together to succeed in completing their task.

*1951*

**5/8 Finished raking** (hay) **today. Went to School of Institute this eve. I was on the kitchen committee.**(extension sponsored seminar)

**5/14 Painted the toilet this morning.**(still using outhouse) ...

**6/1 Did some pressing today. All of us took baths and hair washes.**

**9/28 Roy started to plant wheat this morning. Grandpa Keppy past away about 11:30. Grandma found him in the garden about 12:30. All the kids were in this afternoon. Was a bright day outside.**

Roy did help to some degree with the home renovations, though his attention was focused primarily on getting the other farm buildings in a usable condition. Preparation of the land for planting was his highest priority. Living so close to older brothers, he was offered numerous opinions. But all of their coaching could not surpass the value of his intuition about farming. This was a man who knew how to think things through and see them to completion!

*1952*

**1/31 Daddy had an attack at 6:30 this morning & had several thru the day. He died at 6:30 in the eve. Complete stoppage about 4 times. Was a nice day. We were there all day. Aunt Ruby was here with the boys.**

**2/26 They hauled manure here again today. I washed. Went up to Braack & figured out our will.**

**8/12 Roy got 9ᵗʰ in the market barrow show. There were 45. Had dinner along.**

It became a tradition to share a picnic meal on hog show day at the fair with friends and relatives...and she started it.

**8/14 Today Roy showed purebreds. Did better than he thought.**

Roy had great interest in animal husbandry and a belief in diversity. In the former, he was truly an original thinker – in the latter, a follower of the family farm thinking of the times. Little did they know then that the style and size of farming would change so steadily. Theirs would be out-of-date practically before they were done with it. Yet they plugged away in their own way and achieved remarkable accomplishments.

**9/28 Painted in the spare room this morning & this aft went with Roy & bought some Hampshires.**

**11/4 Election Day—1952. Ike and Stevenson. Ike won. Went to town today and then to Rays kids birthdays. Then to pancake supper & then watched TV at Rays.**

This seemed to be the deciding factor in whether to make the major purchase of a television set—watching election results. TV watching was only acceptable at certain times and for short periods of time. Not only was it generally perceived to be a waste of time, but sitting too close or watching too much would surly damage ones eyes! However, there were many relaxing Sunday evenings watching "The Wonderful World of Disney" followed by "Bonanza" as a family. This was one time during the week that Myrtle tried to stay out of the kitchen, so the fare was simply popcorn, rice, or Campbell's soup.

Two thirds of American homes were equipped with a black and white television by 1955, but it wasn't until Walt Disney produced "The Wonderful World of Color" in the next decade that the Keppys heard the announcement, 'the following program is brought to you in living color'. When color TVs first became available they cost about as much as an average new car.

After the introduction of television to society, the TV dinner was not far behind. These sparse and tasteless frozen meals, along with the infamous pot pies, were the ultimate in convenience foods at the time. They ushered in the era of less fuss in the kitchen in keeping with increasingly less domesticated women.

## 1953

**1/21 Got our television set this afternoon.**

**1/27 Roy and I cut the hog up & Ralph rendered out our lard. Mom and I made sour meat & grit while Roy went to vet Nite School.**

**2/22 Started to go to church services this morning. Went to Grandpa's for their 54th wedding anniv.**

**3/3 Roy and I bought our farm today. Had dinner at Grandmas. Pd. $275**(per acre). **Paid half. Mom was here with boys.**

**3/29 Kids were baptized this morn & Roy and I this afternoon. Mom was out. She also baked cookies and rolls.**

**4/6 I worked in the field most of the day. Boys played in pasture. Roy started to seed oats.**

**4/19 Snowed off and on all day. Roy has been selling sows and gilts for $22.50. Went to Bougarts with Ray's. Boys stayed at Mom. Boys started Sunday School.**

**8/17 Left for DesMoines at 8 this eve on train.** (for Iowa State Fair) **Roy got grand champion market hog today. Also took my things today. Mom stayed with boys.**

**9/16** (Austin—National Barrow Show) **Roy watched judging all day. The ladies com. Took us thru Hormel Inst. And 150,000** (dollar) **house for tea. Roy bought 2 boars-Berkshires.**

**11/24 Roy spent the day at Oscar Mayer to learn more about judging hogs...**

**11/30 Roy and I left at 10 this morning for Chicago. Went to livestock show this afternoon... (stayed at Hilton)**

**12/1 Roy judged the hogs at 10 this morning in Normandie Lounge...**

**12/16 Went shopping while Roy went to swine clinic...**

Pork producers were not organized to promote their product until Roy and Myrtle helped to organize it. Determined to meet the demands of consumers for a meatier piece of meat, he began cross breeding... This required hours of record keeping and even more hours of earmarking and sorting hogs. Myrtle was, of course, right there ready to be of assistance. Together they devised a method to combine 2 sets of purebred hogs' records with the outcome being longer and leaner hogs which were better for breeding and marketing.

Roy said regarding reasons for crossbreeding:

"I went to extension meetings and picked up pieces of information on heterosis. (gene selection) Crossbreeding provided an energy factor—the hogs would grow faster and stronger. I started with Chester White then Yorkshire (for mothering and milking ability).

Wilbur Plager encouraged lean type hogs based on consumer needs. We then looked for growing ability and feed efficiency so we went with Durocs—"born with their mouth open looking for self-feeder"—you could hardly believe your eyes to see how it changed! Why wouldn't you do it? But the judges chose purebreds 1st, 2nd, 3rd,--slick little Berkshires—It was so frustrating when clearly the crossbreds were better!

We used a cooler from Oscar Mayer to display fat market hog vs. lean market hog carcasses for producers to compare at judging contests. Leanard Duman (from Oscar Mayer) was training at the same time. First judged from magazine and won trip to Palmer House ballroom (Chicago). "It seemed simple, but I changed my mind because others were taking so long."

Roy said, "It was disheartening to know you had it, but judges couldn't see it. Went again to National Barrow Show Market Hog judging contest and persisted because, "You have to do what you think is right or get pushed around..." Finally, in 1960 1st Nat. Barrow Show Crossbred Champion. Then in '62, 1st crossbred champs at International Livestock Exposition in Chicago (competing with hogs from all over the world). Afterwards, "old pig farmers squeezed my hand so hard I could feel bone crushing...and then they came...from all over the world to see how we did it on the farm." It was strawberry picking time, they brought us some, I can see the old black car come down the road, 'just wanted to see if what he said was true about the farm--

- it was an endless stream...unbelievable!" ...Just wish we'd written more down ."(assured him it was being written now)

## *1954*

As her story progresses, fewer diary entries seem to be about herself and more about Roy and farm life. This is consistent with Myrtle's 'supporting role' in the ongoing drama of her rural reality.

## 1/1...paid off our farm today.

My Farm, a poem Myrtle read at a Farm Bureau meeting and then submitted to that organization's paper captures the sense of owning a farm:

> "*I bought ten thousand sunsets*
> *and a friendly old oak tree*
> *and jeweled nets of violets*
> *when my farm was deeded to me...*
> *...The owner thought he sold me land;*
> *How poor a trader he!*
> *But it was all fair, for it all was there*
> *For all the world to see...*
> *... I paid the man his money*
> *and he did not understand*
> *That he put a price on Paradise*
> *When he thought he sold me land.*"
> Author Unknown

Myrtle became pregnant again. Delivering a girl was quite a surprise since most relatives had whole families of boys or girls, but not both. Always conscious of recycling, her first reaction was, "Now what will we do with all the boys' clothes?" They were so unprepared for a girl that they had no idea what to name her. Roy heard the name they chose on the radio while driving past his own birthplace (Charlie's farm) in to the hospital to visit

Myrtle and their 3 day old daughter. He said Dorothy Dengler came to watch the boys and take care of the little chicks hatched at the same time and "we got them big, too."

**2/5 Had labor pain all thru nite & morning. Went to St. Lukes about 2:30. Annette was born at 7:59...**

**3/6 Roy drove to Cedar Rapids hog show today...**

**3/20 Was at Hog Show all day...Roy got 5 blues out of six.**

**3/24...Had ham which Roy won for carcass judging.**

**4/4 Annette was baptized this morning. Roy started in field this afternoon. Ozark airlines started today at Mt.Joy airport.**

**4/11 Had a Keppy party here today. Went to church this morning because it was 1ˢᵗ anniversary.** (of the church)

*"As you close your eyes in slumber, do you think that God will say; 'You have earned one more tomorrow by the work you did today?'" Author Unknown*

In this quote from another favorite poem of Myrtle's, her Protestant work ethic is loud and clear. Though charter members of the fledgling Lutheran church in Eldridge, she didn't seem to trust Luther's emphasis on 'grace through faith...not by works alone'. Her perceived need to earn her way to the next day was evident every day, though her spirituality was somewhat elusive. As a young girl, she occasionally attended the Presbyterian Church on the corner where she lived. Then as a young woman, she and Roy, and their two little boys were baptized as a family at Faith Lutheran Church.

**4/18 Easter. Went to church. Took communion & then to Grandma K. for dinner. then to Fej park. Went to S.S.**(Sunday School) **program tonite. Mom stayed with Annette as she has a bad cold.**

**6/17 Went to National Livestock & Meat Board mtg. at Conrad Hilton** (Chicago) **Had banquet there this eve. Afterwards walk to Lake & went to Pomp room.**

**12/22 Decorated our tree this eve. Dressed ducks and geese today**.

This, of course, did not mean putting clothes on the fowl!

*1955*

**1/17 Washed this morning. Annette in for smallpox vac. & Mom and I went to Kuhl. Roy and I went to mtg. in Bett. For F.B.**

**2/25...Annette is getting chicken pox**

**8/19 Roy and Glen was to fair this afternoon. Roy got first on Yorkshire boar.**

It was frustrating at times for Roy to get the right boars. Hamps, for example, were more gruff— some sows would jump up and step on babies.

**9/30 ...Took Annette to Dr. & she had toxin impetigo**

Though vaccinations were becoming available, many potentially serious illnesses were a fact of life. Polio was widespread until the immunization was required in the fifties.

Little did Myrtle know that before long a situation that she never even considered would absorb her body, mind and spirit, creating a memory she would try unsuccessfully to forget.

# Chapter Six
# "An Unhappy Birth and Another Baby Girl"

Myrtle's fifth FIVE YEAR DIARY is held together with disintegrating tape, pages loose and torn. It is prefaced by these thoughts:

"Memory is Elusive—Capture It—The mind is a wonderful machine. It need but just be refreshed and incidents can again be revived in their former clarity. A line each day, whether it be important substances, will in time to come bring back those vague memories, worth remembering, to almost actual reality. Five years of your life, in written form, will be your reward for keeping this book faithfully and accurately. You will record your daily habits, your thoughts and events of importance. As you round out this chronicle of your doings, you will be able to check back a year from the time you are writing, and see at a glance your activities of a year ago. As you go along, you will be able to turn aside the veil of forgetfulness, and see the events of two, three and even four years ago. You will find amusing recollections that will bring chuckles—possibly business affairs whose record will prove valuable, and certainly little precious memories that you will want to keep in the permanent form which this book provides.".

Myrtle often did use her diaries in the ways suggested, even if it was just to satisfy a curiosity about what the weather was like on the same date in preceding years. The cumulative wealth of data from many years of diaries is another story.

After two years, Myrtle became pregnant again, but this time it was not a happy birth. The baby was overdue and had suffered heart complications before passing on

58

moments after birth. They named her Royce Adell after themselves, and purchased a cemetery plot for her to be buried. In October of 2003, Myrtle shared some more thoughts about their baby who was born still, "Mother had to make me more maternity clothes because I got so big by August but she wasn't born until October. They think it was dead that whole time, but I didn't cause there was so much extra water she moved around, probably a blessing. When she finally was born, they had to tie me down cause I wanted so badly to hold her. That was awful!

Roy and the boys (ages 7 and 9) came into the hospital and cried and cried. It was so sad. They dressed her and we bought a little casket and burial plot... They could have let me hold her. That wasn't right!" This loss of opportunity to hold their child is the biggest regret of her life, as any woman who has given birth will understand. Though surely done at the time to protect from heartbreaking emotion, this natural part of the grieving process is now better understood and parents are no longer prevented from permission to privately mourn and hold a stillborn baby.

The sadness over this loss was not openly experienced for long. They had to quickly 'get over it' and carry on, as there remained much to be done. Their marriage understandably suffered strain at this point.

**1956**

**10/8 Cleaned upstairs & got the baby clothes out today.**

**10/19 Was in delivery room 2 hrs. Royce Adell was still born at 9:14. Had kindy rough nite. funeral**

**10/31—11/2 packed away baby clothes**

**12/16 Put wreath on baby's grave. Went to Moline airport to see Rose Bowl football team off.** (Iowa beat Oregon--earlier, greeted golf champ at Mt.Joy--Arnold Palmer)

Their two year old daughter did end up wearing some of the boys' old clothes for 'everyday', but she also had her picture taken in frilly dresses. They even won 2nd place at a masquerade contest with her in an outfit they created for St. Patrick's Day when she was 3. Though Myrtle tried hard to keep her daughter indoors learning 'women's work', the little girl had a need to be outside with her dad feeding the animals and working the fields. This was a disappointment for Myrtle, but a joy for Roy.

**1957**

**2/3 Took kids to SS.**(Sunday School) **Grandma E. Clifford &Aunt Ruby were here for duck dinner for Annette's birthday.**

**2/4 Had Mother's Club this afternoon. Rays and Charlies were here this eve for Ann. Birthday. She went home with them.**

**3/9 Went to hog show. Roy got grand and reserve champion and second on judging. Went to Walcott Masquerade and Ann. was a shamrock and got second.**

**3/26 Grandma K. died this morning. We all went in. She was not ready tonite. Annette stayed at Ruby's.**

**4/15 Washed today. My wringer broke so had to wring it out by hand. Roy finished seeding oats.**

**1958**

**3/1 Roy won champion truckload today. He got a silver tray** (in Cedar Rapids)

This was the first of several silver trays awarded for champions which were later used proudly to serve ham sandwiches to special guests.

**9/2 Left at 10:30 for Chicago. Mom and kids went along. Went to Brookfield Zoo this afternoon. Stayed at Capperallo.**

**9/3 Sold steers at $27.50 at 1380** (lbs.) **at eleven.** (Morning sales signified the buyer's choice of all cattle brought to the stockyards for sale that day.)**Then went to** (Museum of) **Science and Industry. Ate at Forest Inn on the way home. Roy went to ele mtg.**(elevator meeting for grain cooperative)

**12/8 Had swine producers mtg at Walt Schneckloths this eve. Kids stayed home alone.**

Then, to their delight, another girl was born to them. She was a lively little one that all her siblings doted on—truly 'the baby of the family'. She was brought home from the hospital on Easter Day, likc a gift from God. Henceforth, the family existed as 'the boys' and 'the girls' though the differences in each category were pronounced. A family meal became a real deal!

Each child had their invisibly labeled seat at the table for meals. The girls served and cleaned up while the boys talked farming. The girls had trouble getting a word in edgewise. There was kicking under the table and nasty looks shot like arrows. An excellent cook, Myrtle specialized in creative use of leftovers for the family meals. Though the 'icebox' and freezer were always filled to the brim, not to mention a full canning cellar, the selection on the table was often rather slim. Dinner was the main meal at noon, so supper was sort of an afterthought. The kids could look forward to a substantial after school snack—often something fresh baked, like her thick and gooey rhubarb dessert that tasted like spring itself. She usually prepared mid morning 'lunch', possibly open-faced egg salad sandwiches and lemonade or coffee, for the men in the fields, which was always received with great appreciation. It gave her a chance to get outside or send one of the girls as they grew.

**1959**

**2/10 No school because of sleet storm. Mr. Listke from Minnesota brought Roys 2 Yorkshire boars.**

**3/6 Dale and Annette got measles.**

**3/24 Woke up with a discharge this morn. Left for hospital at 10. Ila Jean was born at 2:59. Was out most of the night. High was 72 degrees.**

**4/9 Mom took Annette to dancing lessons...**

**5/1 Oscar Mayer and his son were here this morning. Ila Jean got sick again toward eve. They took Leonard Duman to hospital.**

Roy and Myrtle became friends with Leonard and Lucille Duman and other Oscar Mayer employees, including Oscar Mayer himself. Familiarizing themselves with better production methods resulted in the leaner product demanded by pork consumers. Lard, or melted down and resolidified hog fat, had been in great demand during the war as a lubricant for the moving parts of guns. Homemakers also learned to use purified lard in place of scarce butter as a shortening for making delicious pie crusts and cookies. When the war ended, however, the need for lard decreased significantly.

Before long, the healthfulness of such consumption of animal fats was questioned and its usage decreased. Soon, leaner hogs with less backfat were in demand and packing plants like Oscar Mayer tried to respond by training producers to reach that goal. Making changes in breeding and feeding were encouraged, of which Roy was a forerunner.

He hired a young man who became like part of the family as he daily worked beside Roy on the farm for many years. Myrtle agreed to 'feed' the new hired man during the day. Along with the children and Myrtle, Leon's presence made it possible for Roy to be away from the farm as needed for promotional and political events.

**6/1 Leon started for good. I washed.**

**6/9 Annette and I went to Rae Dance Studio Revue this eve. They made hay.**

**6/21 Roy went to S.S. with kids. Ann. Got scared when she was to say her piece...**

**7/6 Left at 11:30 for Wagon Wheel. Mom stayed here with Ila Jean. Got there about 5. Went swimming and bowling this eve.**

**7/7 Kids all went swimming & later the kids and Roy went horseback riding.**

**7/24 Roy fell off baler trailer this aft. Straw. They finished combining. It run over both legs.**

This accident occurred while waves of visible heat rippled over the dark earth of the Iowa hay fields, which had become hard and cracked during a period of drought. All longed for the coolness of the predicted thunderstorms. The straw was dry and had to be hoisted into the barn before the rain fell. There was no time to pause for a drink of lemonade brought to the field by a little daughter who was waved away, while at the same time the nearly full wagon hit a bump as the tractor slowed and Roy fell forward. He disappeared under the wagon before the tractor could be stopped! Turning in her tracks, the drink deliverer raced as fast as her short little legs and bare feet could carry her across the sharp stubble, shouting out for help. Myrtle quickly called for an ambulance and drove the car to the field to comfort Roy in the meantime.

**1960**

**1/26 Took Ann dancing as she is taking private lessons now. Roy cut up hog. I brought meat in & brought Mom out as we went out with George and Janice.**

**1/27 Rendered out 3 gallons lard and made grit vouse. Went to P.T.A. mtg. tonite.**

**3/12 Went to club at Carolyns. Annette** (written herself) **lost her 1st tooth...**

**9/16...Roy had grand champ truckload of show** (Austin)...

The previous year, Roy had been advised to go to the National Barrow Show in Austin 'just to look first once'. Myrtle went along since she had heard there was a ladies program. But when she tried to register in the Ladies Building they asked her which breed of hogs her husband showed. To her response of crossbred she was abruptly told, "Oh, we don't have no crossbreds here!" She says, "I remember that so well. So when permitted to exhibit crossbreds the following year, my mother said, "Oh Girl, no!", hoping to spare her repeated rejection. But instead they surprised many with their first top prize at the show!

Between meals, Myrtle often spent time talking with friends or relatives who stopped by, or by phone.

The first phone Myrtle and Roy had hung on the wall in the kitchen. A large wooden box with a black mouthpiece that stuck out and a long black earpiece on a cord, it was 'a far cry' from the pocket sized cellular phones now in use! It was a party line shared by about 12 other families. If you 'picked up' while they were on the line you could listen in—and you knew they could listen to you, too. It was easy to complain about someone staying on too long by simply picking up and listening in until noticed, particularly interesting if it were a young niece rambling on with her boyfriend.

There was a neighborhood group that gathered socially. Myrtle and Roy also became members of several card groups, the main ones usually referred to as 'Little Club" and 'Big Club'. Myrtle made sure the children were included in holiday picnics with these groups. Any gathering always included food. Hot German potato salad was one of her specialties, as were pecan pie, ham rollups and an endless array of Jello salad combinations. So adept in the kitchen that she just knew how to make something taste delicious, Myrtle cooked primarily by adding a pinch of this or a handful of that!

Roy would eat anything (except fish of any kind), so he was the taste tester for new recipes she conjured up. Many of these were never written down, but have been repeated through the years. When there was an abundance of tart cherries from the tree in the backyard, she made cherry soup. If the sweet corn was plentiful, that might be all she served for supper. Roasting a variety of cuts of meat (including beef tongue) with whatever veggies were available and lots of potatoes rounded out her recipe repertoire.

Quite a large vegetable garden became a family project. It began with planting potatoes on Good Friday. Then the tomato plants were set out. After that, rows and rows of tiny seeds were planted that emerged as radishes, lettuce, carrots, beets, peas, beans and zinnias. Of course, the garden needed regular hoeing to keep the weeds at bay. And when something needed harvesting it had to be dealt with--usually canned or frozen, but often given away. It was difficult to predict crop yield, but it always seemed there was more than plenty.

Roy took great interest in cross breeding – not only hogs, but Indian Corn and zinnias, too. He would save seeds from the best plants with certain colors and try to cross them the following year with remarkable results! Many of these hybrids were entered at the county fair. They started making and sharing decorative swags by bundling 3 ears of colorful corn together and tying with baler twine. This became quite an autumn accomplishment as it grew into a garage industry in later years. Their corn bundles were popular and sold quickly through a local grocer.

# Section 3

# Chapter Seven
# "The Children Molded, The House Remodeled"

*"The melody of each generation emerges from all that's gone before."* Fred Rogers

The next diary is inscribed as "The Property of Roy B. Keppy family". This seems to be recognition of the value of the diary as a historical document representative of the whole family. It also includes the scribbles of the kids imitating their mother's regular writing in this little book.

Myrtle had beautiful handwriting. After many years of deterioration, these books are easier to read in sunshine (especially the portions written in pencil). Her busy life during these years and disorderly household in the midst of construction is apparent by the many ink colors used, whatever was handy when she actually found time to sit down and write. It turns out to be helpful when each year on a page is a different color.

**1961**

**1/6 ...Was 54 degrees.(**January thaw)

**1/13 ... Was 57 degrees...**

**1/20 ... Turning cold. Below Zero...**

**1/15 Went to see 'Ben Hur' this aft. & then bought Pizza & ate supper at Moms.**

**1/16 Went to town & helped Mom buy a Rambler. Roy went to Felco** (livestock feed Co.) **supper & boys to basketball practice.**

**2/5 Had Annette and Walt's birthday here today for the aft. 35 were here. Was a nice day.**

**3/9 Lard baking contest. Glen got reserve pig.** (second place of all pigs entered) **Went to banquet at Wash. With Knowles this eve. Had a few experiences.**

Myrtle helped to organize the Scott County Lard Baking contest to encourage the use of lard in baking.

**3/15... Roy had to go to court this eve as he got picked up for speeding. Cost $9.85.**

**9/28 Left at 1:30 for Sauk City for Yorkshire sale. Roy bought two gilts. Wilbur gave me green slacks. Stayed at motel. (**Note: she never wore slacks—was he trying to suggest it?)

Myrtle had a seemingly endless supply of 'everyday' dresses, which she literally wore every day. From polka dots and stripes to paisley and floral prints, her dresses were worn until threadbare.

During Myrtle's childhood and early married years, she was often of meager means. This privation shaped her lifestyle then and surely affected her personality and frugal approach to life. Her need to wear out items before replacing them meant that some replacement items, such as towels and an electric frying pan, remained new and in their packaging for years. Something purchased new had to stay in the box or hang in the closet for a time before being worn, so as to not take for granted its newness!

**1962**

**1/9 No school. Cold and snow blowing. Really cold. The highest was 5 below zero.** What a difference a year can make in the weather:

**3/1 ... coldest since 1891.**

**11/27 Big Day. Roy showed champ. Barrow at about 2:30. Quite exciting...**
He says this was his first really big win because it was a true international show.

**12/14 Washed my first load of clothes in my new washer. Shorty** (great nickname for a short electrician) **pretty well finished here in kitchen and family room. Took Annette dancing at Poor farm.** (Home of the elderly and disabled)

By the end of 1962, much of Myrtle's life literally came up out of the cellar. With the installation of a new utility room on the main floor, doing the laundry became downright convenient. She continued doing only the dirty overalls in the basement and hanging most clothes on the line outside, or all over the chairs in the house in inclement weather, to save the new machines. In the big picture of her household responsibilities, this move saved her numerous steps and kept her closer to that all important telephone. Even after the advent of more wash-and-wear fabrics, she continued to iron nearly everything—including sheets and underwear— sometimes balling it up dampened until she could get to it, by which time it may no longer have smelled so fresh. Fabrics softening dryer sheets were not a part of her laundering system.

**12/16 Worked all day. Got ready to move into new kitchen. Ate our first meal in new kitchen after coming home from S.S. program.**

The home addition and remodeling took a great deal of time, energy and money throughout the years '61-'62. Roy's cousin, Ray Danielson did much of the work, but the electrician and plumber (Red) were frequently there as well as the drape lady, carpet layers, plasterers, etc. Many problems occurred: such as the new septic tank caving in, the kitchen counter breaking and having to be reordered 3 times, temporary pipes freezing, etc. But the family survived by 'living' in whatever parts of the house were not currently being worked on and the outcome was quite an improvement!

**1963**

Before long, the family moved out of the dining room and living room and took the plaster off of both rooms. They became suddenly and annoyingly inundated with billions of big bad wolf spiders!

**2/13 Baked bread, pies, cookies today. Roy went to livestock school. Danielsons & the stereo man were out this eve.**

**2/20 Roy went to swine clinic today. Max Whitaker gave the lesson. I finished our bedroom drapes.** (She sewed them herself.)

**3/7 I baked all 6 things & got 3rd prize on my tea ring. Got reserve lite wt hog. Annette & Roy went to Brownies date nite at Masonic temple.** (Spring Market Hog Show & Lard Baking contest at the Mississippi Valley Fairgrounds—they helped to create this event and supported it through the years)

**3/16 Roy was a judge at Kewanee hog show. Went to 4-H basketball this eve.**

**3/21 Had club at Elnora's this aft. This eve had cancer mtg. at church. Roy went to F.B. breakfast this morn.**

**4/1 Went to cancer mtg. this morn. Leon started to plow oats this aft. Roy & boys went to FFA** (Future Farmers of America) **carcass show. The one Roy judged at. (**LowMoor**)**

**6/16 Charlies, Rays, Grandma & Aunt Ruby & us went to Longview** (park in Moline) **& cooked our breakfast. We stayed for swimming & ate supper there to.**

**6/23 Left this morn for Ames as Roy was a judge at Yorkshire picnic at Plagers. Stayed at Holiday Inn.**

**6/29 Roy was a judge at Poland China** (a breed of hog) **picnic at Ames today. Boys went to Church Camp. Grandma stayed here with girls.**

**9/30 Roy had to give a talk to some men for pork promotion this eve. I started to clean the garage. I helped address Sister papers.**

**11/14 It was announced today that Roy won the Ford Almanac award. He had to go to T.V. station WQAD & appear. Got our new office chair.**

Myrtle and Roy accomplished much of their extensive office work at this desk in their family room.

**11/19 Delivered 180 pumpkins to Masonic Temple for 4-H youth banquet which we went to.**

**11/22 Kennedy was assinated in Texas this noon...**

**12/2 Roy showed the grand champion truckload of 10 head today...** at the International Livestock Exposition in Chicago

**12/30 Roy and Dale went to WMT to make T.V. tape for livestock judging contest. Glen went to Ext. office for interview. I went to FB mtg. Had Xmas at Grandmas for supper.**

**12/31 ...Went to Ikes Grove this eve. Went to Leonard and Lois first. Grandma and kids went to Mary Denglers.**

Ikes Grove is short for Isaacs Walton League, a conservation lodge nearby with picnic space and clay bird shooting range. Many events were held here including holiday parties, July 4th fireworks, and even wedding receptions.

Mary Dengler was Roy's sister who lived in a big farmhouse with a player piano. She was a very large gracious woman (glandular imbalance) who hosted the whole Keppy family (sometimes about 50 people) for New Years Eve. Potluck plus frueden, fun and games with the country cousins...and special music from the pedal player piano!

**1964**

**1/1 New Years at Charlies. Had turkey. Was a real nice day.** (Roy's brother who lived just around the corner on the Keppy home place.)

**2/1 Had 16 girls here for Annettes birthday. Was a nice day... doll cake, favors**

**2/6** (Louisville. KY) **Roy had champ and reserve champ crossbred pigs & champion truckload. Took the hamp people out for supper & then went around town with Plagers and Ebbings.**

**2/10 Got a letter from Ford Co. telling us we are awarded a trip to the World's Fair. Roy sold some hogs.**

**2/22 They** (Roy and the boys) **came home from Albert Lea** (MN) **about midnite. They brought home 3 silver trays & a big trophy...**

**3/7 Girls, Grandma and I left for C.R.** (Cedar Rapids) **hog show. Roy had champion ind. & truckload. Glen had the champ 4-H pig. Duman, Cress, Knowles & Charlies were here awhile this eve.** (Sounds like a party!)

**5/17 ...Put feathers in pillows today.** (duck and goose feathers from fowl she raised)

**5/19 They started to take down buggy shed at other farm... they finished building the 3ʳᵈ shade rack from buggy shed.** (masterful recycling!)

**5/28 Roy started his Dale Carnegie course.**

**7/7 We got 2 ½ inches of rain in a bad storm. It blew corn and oats down. Picked up apricots at Fryes this eve. Charlies big tree in field burned.** (lightning)

**9/25 3 fellows from the Canadian Broadcasting Co. spent 11 hrs. here today to do some filming...**

**11/14 Took Annette to Dr again & she has serious gland infection...**

Shifting from relatively mundane happenings to somewhat more significant events of the day characterize Myrtle's diary entries through these middle years of her life. In fact, she may have clung to the mundane to have survived the significant.

**1965**

**1/12 Annette had her first organ lesson. Girls and I went shopping at Plaza.**

**1/31 Brought York boar out to Beryl Keen & got Duroc boar. Run into bad snowstorm on way out. My picture was in paper on Mrs. Section.**

Quad City Times entitled "After the pigs, I come first!" This referred in part to the fact that they put air conditioners in the hog barns before the house.

**3/7 Dale took girls to SS & church. Charlies, Dumans & us went for dinner to Bishops. Kids went bowling & roller skating.**

**4/14 We all went down this eve to help fill sand bags.** (Mississippi River flooding) **It kindy** (kind of) **rained all day.**

**4/21 ...Grandma Wiese died this eve at 5:30. She had been in a coma since Sunday.**

**7/9 Went out to Devil's Lake & cooked breakfast & dinner there. Kids swam. Rode the "Ducks" at Dells & visited Deer Park Trout Farm. Ate at Paul Bunyans this eve.**

**9/16 Roy had champion truckload this morning & champion barrow this aft. Was real exciting. Was cold and damp. Started home at 5:30** (National Barrow Show—where Roy has shown the most champions of any since it began)

**10/2 There were fellows here from Sweden this aft...**

**10/12 A fellow from Argentina came this aft & stayed overnite.**

Regarding visitors to the farm, the many "pork people" were regular visitors, often bringing international farmers, professors in agriculture and/or international dignitaries. An impressive collection of autographs was kept in a guest book which was misplaced.

**12/29 Left at 10:30 for Chicago to see our** (Champion) **pig at Lincoln Zoo. We went to see Barefoot in the Park stage play this eve.**

**1966**

**1/25 Boys both pinned their men at wrestling with Bettendorf. Real exciting. Roy was on panel at Atkinson Illinois this eve.**

**2/1 Took Roy over to airport as he has to give talk in Lansing Michigan tomorrow. Bought Annette some skates on way home.**

**4/3 Had company off and on all day today. Sold gilts and oats this morn. Roy called from Texas this eve. Was 80 degrees there and 40 here?**

**4/10 Easter. Boys went to sun rise services at Eldridge & Wharton Field House. We went to Sound of Music this aft. Had supper at Grandmas.**

**7/13 Ila Jean had her dance lesson. Elnora and I went for our class. Served at the last 4-H ball game this eve. Hugo Timm was here from Texas. There were fellows here from Phillapines.**

**8/27 Were awarded Iowa Blue Ribbon Family. Was a hot day. Was honored on adm. steps & in the grandstand. Stayed at Ames. Went to Bernard Collins 25<sup>th</sup> anniv party this eve. Took Whitakers along. Glen came home earlier as he escorted the Herman & the Hermits.**

Picture of the family in front of 'the trophy case'.

The Roy B. Keppy family of R.R. #3, Davenport—Ila Jean, Glen, Mrs. Keppy, Mr. Keppy, Dale, and Annette—who received the Iowa State Fair's highest honor by being named Iowa's 1966 Blue

Of the many awards received by the family, this may have been the one most meaningful, as it represented cumulative success and included the whole family.

**10/31 The guys had elevator mtg. & while they were there us gals had a Halloween party at the new building. Took girls trick or treat tonite. They took yield & said it was 172.** (bushels per acre)

Halloween treats were more substantial in the country, but walking from house to house for treats in town was a good reason for Myrtle to visit her mother.

## 1967

**4/23 Had a snow storm today. Left 2 inches. Glen went back to college this eve. I drove kids to S.S.**

**5/20 Went out with Kardels & Paustians tonite. We all had our corn in.** (Planted)

Celebrations of seasonal accomplishments were common, since the end of planting or after the harvest did require a sigh of relief following such intensity. August, however, was a month of fairgoing—first the Mississippi Valley Fair in Davenport then the Iowa State Fair in DesMoines.

**8/19** (Iowa State Fair) **Dale had the champion litter. Annette the champion pen and individual. Was a big day. Annette rode around in the fire wagon.** (with her champion pig in front of the grandstand) **Went across the street for supper tonight.**

Going to supper at a nice restaurant signified a special occasion. The place across the street from the hog barn at the State Fair grounds was quite handy when the day was long and 'fair' food no longer satisfied.

**9/12 Rained hard all day in Austin. Roy showed 1ˢᵗ in LW & MW and 2ⁿᵈ in LW.** (lightweight and middle weight hogs) **I went to luncheon today. Roy drove our freak pig in crossbred drive. Went out with Plager this eve.**

Always one to draw a laugh when he could, Roy couldn't resist 'showing' this pig that didn't have enough ribs. Demonstrating exactly the opposite of the ' length and strength' he preached for better meat type hogs, this little pig was a perfect presentation—prompting not only many laughs, but also lively discussion.

**9/29 Today was the mtg at the Florida experiment farm at Live Oak. Was a good day & crowd. Roy gave a talk this morn and afternoon. Tonight we stayed at Daytona Beach. Ate supper overlooking ocean & there was a storm.**

The rest of this story is that the rental car they drove down to the water's edge sunk in the sand as the tide came in!

**11/29 We left at 4:30 for Louisville Ken. For Nat. Pork P. Council Mtg. Hamans and Einfelds went with us. Had banquet this eve. Roy had mtg till midnite. I gave report.**

The report Myrtle gave was the culmination of an extensive research project done by the Porkettes. She really relished her leadership role in this auxiliary organization of the Pork Producers. It gave her the opportunity to travel (often with Roy) and to make many friends, always reaching out to new members. She worked effectively with nutritionists and marketers, clearly articulating her opinions without being overbearing. Her example is one to follow.

**1968**

**1/17 I left this morn for Des Moines with** (Pork) **Queen & her Mother. Went to banquet this eve and to dance. Went to eat afterwards & went without coats as it was real warm.**

**3/22 There was a busload of kindergarten from Bettendorf here today. Oats customers also. The boys came home** (from college) **for the weekend.**

It must have felt like the house had a revolving door at times, the way people would come and go!

**4/5 Went to FB day in Eldridge this aft. Martin Luther King was shot in Memphis today. Dale hitch hiked home this afternoon. We went to play this eve.**

**6/12 I had Porkette mtg at O'Hara Inn.** (Chicago) **Roy & girls sold steers. Then we went to stay at Pheasant Run.**

**6/13 Girls and Roy went swimming in indoor & outdoor pool. Picked up our wooden pig at Algonquin this aft. Visited Johnny Hildebrand. Went to stay at Wagon Wheel.**

Family vacations were always arranged around some other reason to travel—fairs, buying hogs, selling steers, or pork meetings. Though Roy and Myrtle took swimming lessons together, even after that she rarely got in to swim, but always looked for opportunities for the rest of the family to enjoy a dip.

**11/5 Big and exciting election. Humphrey & Nixon as the winner. Went to Dr. White & ate supper & then to Susans to watch election returns for awhile. Roy had elevator mtg.**

**11/27 Annette and Roy left at 11 this morn for International. I made pumpkin & nut bread this afternoon.**

**12/27 Went into Grandmas for ham supper this eve. Rained some again. Annette is working on scrapbook. The men came back from visiting the moon.**

**1969**

**1/1 Went up to Rays for goose dinner. Ila Jean had got sick during the nite at Dave K. & stayed down until 5 this aft & then got up. Bonnie and Charlie were also sick. Hong Kong flu going around.**

**1/19 Went to church as Roy ushered. Annette went to see Gone With the Wind. Worked most of the day.**

**1970**
**5/8 67 kids were out from Grant school this morn. Got my eyes examined this noon and got my hair fixed.**

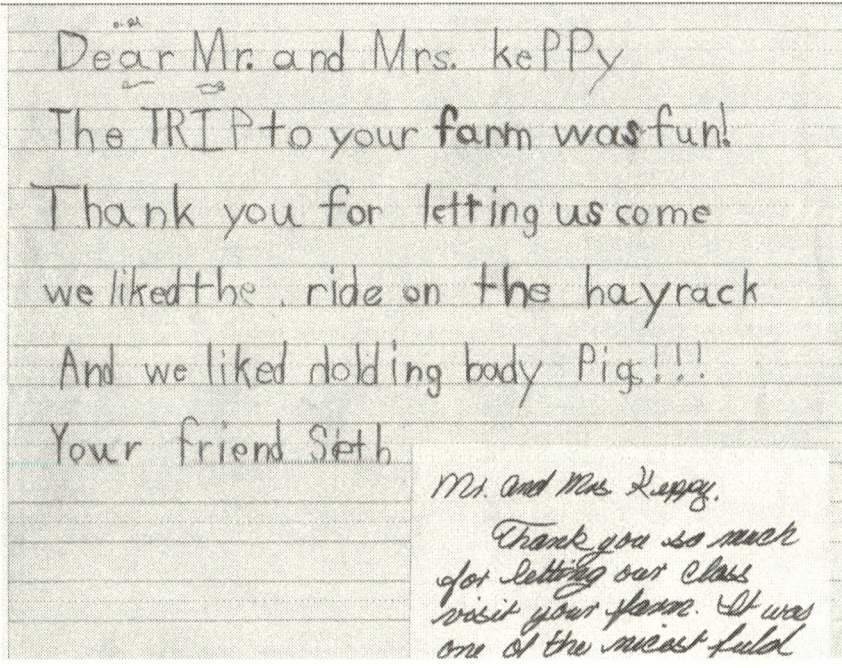

Dear Mr. and Mrs. kePPy
The TRIP to your farm was fun!
Thank you for letting us come
we liked the ride on the hayrack
And we liked dolding body Pig!!!
Your friend Seth

Mr. and Mrs. Keppy.
Thank you so much
for letting our class
visit your farm. It was
one of the nicest field

**9/5 Roy judged at the Minnesota State Fair all day, the FFA show. We met the Forshlers & they took girls on rides & things & ate at the fairgrounds. Annette & Grandma to show- Art Linkletter.**

# Chapter Eight
# "Champion Parties in Remodeled Home"

*"What can we make of our parents, grandparents, the networks of kin who constitute our tribal past?"* Ker Conway

Some of these entries give just a sampling of political and public acknowledgements of the unique work Myrtle and Roy were doing for the industry. All of the travel and media attention, as well as public appearances took a great deal of time and energy, but they were like the Energizer bunnies...they just kept going and going and going!

Myrtle was always involved. She often tried to remain in the background, managing correspondence and scheduling speaking engagements. If a person or group (or son or daughter) wanted to meet with Roy, they had to check his schedule first through his wife. The family calendars during those years resembled crossword puzzles!

All the interest in the movement created primarily by the Pork Producers drew the attention of policy makers.

**1971**

**3/8 Roy got an invitation to go to the White House to witness signing bill.** (which he had helped to formulate)

**3/10 Saw Nixon &** (Representative) **Hardin & shook their hands. He went to visit Schwengel & Plambeck. Came home at 8 this eve.**

**5/1 They started to plant again after a much needed rain a few days ago. Got our official notice to come to White House.**

**5/7 Great Day. Salute to Agriculture Day. We were at mtg this morn. Mrs. Hardin hostessed lunch. Mrs. Agnew tea & reception and dance in the White House until 1:30.**
Myrtle remembers, "We danced in the White House to the music of Glen Campbell.

**7/3 Big day at Centennial. We had a float in the parade. 100 years of progress with Pork. Got 3ʳᵈ.**
This family project float consisted of a pen with a wild pig from Texas contrasted with a meat-type hog from their farm to show the progress made.

**7/9 Had 50 Head Start kids here this morn. Roy worked in garden. I picked and made preserves from our apricots.**
One would think having that many kids there was enough for one day, but the other work probably served as therapy to recover from such a visit!

**8/21 Left Columbus about 9 this morn. Went to see Lake Erie & then to get peaches in Michigan & then to Dales. Got ticket.** (speeding)

**10/13 Took Roy over to airport & he went to Wash DC for another mtg & then to reception at White House with Nixon.**

The story continues, additional layers of activity added over the existing busy schedules. How long would Roy and Myrtle persist in the pleasantries of political involvement? Could it get any more interesting or exciting?

**1972**

**1/8 Spent the day at Disney World. Great. Drove to St. Petersburg this eve. Was warm.**

**3/30 It snowed quite hard today. CBS had Roy, Luby** (an economist with Oscar Mayer Co.) **& OM** (Oscar Mayer) **on Walter Cronkite program.**

**8/18 Left at six as girls showed hogs. Ann got 1ˢᵗ commercial gilt. Saw Sonny & Cher this eve.**

**9/23 Went to Des Moines for breakfast with** (Secretary of Agriculture) **Butz &** (Iowa Governor) **Ray.**

**1973**

**1/22 Took Roy to airport as he goes to Nebr for a few days. It was bad weather across the country.**

**2/13 Left at 8 this morn for New Orleans. Roy had mtg. at 1. Went on bourbon st this eve**

**2/25 Started to make grit vouse this morn. Martha, Mary & Anna stopped for dinner. Went to Ila Jeans glee club. Dale came thru and cut up meat this eve.**

**3/24 Had Grandma, Aunt Ruby, Cliffords, Charlies, Rays, Glens here for pork chop dinner.**

**4/22 Easter. Was a half way nice day. Went to sunrise service at church & breakfast. Had goose dinner at Grandmas.**

**6/27 Made 20 lbs of porkburgers for ball games. Roy left for NPPC** (National Pork Producers Council) **mtg in Des Moines.**

**Myrtle and Annette**

**1973**

**7/13 Achievement Show. Annette worked for Pork Producers at Turnstyle. Had visitors from Poland, Yug & Argentina. Got Roy from airport from Springfield.**

**11/7 Left this morn for Phoenix. Freddies met us. Roy judged at Fair & everyone came out there.**

**11/22 Thanksgiving. We finished picking corn. Went to turkey supper at Cliffords. Dales were home.**

**12/4 Got Roy home from Memphis & took him right to elevator mtg.**

## 1974

**2/19 Left for N Carolina. Roy Judge hogs at Smithfield. Stayed at Holiday Inn. Banquet this eve.**

**3/12 Worked on Porkette mailing today. Was on sister school of instruction lunch comm.**

**8/21 Left motel at 4:30 at Westport, Wash & went salmon fishing. Fun. Roy caught 2. Drove back to Seattle this eve and stayed at Thunderbird.**

**9/30 Took Roy over to airport to go to N.P.P.C. mtg in K.C. 40 college kids from Illinois here for tour.**

**10/28 Worked at** (Representative) **Leachs office this aft. Made pear jelly today**.

**11/21 Roy went to Olympic Games at YMCA for rotary. Ila Jean had 4-H mtg. I went to craft class.**

Always very 'crafty', Myrtle had some fun going to classes at Jeanette's (Ray's wife). There she picked up numerous ideas and made gifts galore.

**11/25 Girls, Jean & I ate breakfast by tree at Marshall Fields. We left for home at 2. Was snowing again**. (in Chicago)

Though going to the International Livestock Exposition in Chicago often interfered with Thanksgiving meals at Clifford and Dorothy's, it usually included kicking off the Christmas season with a meal by the huge tree at Marshall Fields. Myrtle knew her way around downtown, and a tour of the store windows was a real thrill!

**12/31 Went to Grandmas for dinner. To Jack Harms for New Years. Laid carpet a Grandmas bathroom.**

Myrtle and the family spent a lot of time with her mother, Mildred, who was widowed quite young. Many stops were made to her little house on Lombard St.— where she always had real cold water in a jar from the icebox, fresh cookies and a deck of cards handy. Projects were often part of the visit. Mildred was way ahead of being environmentally friendly with her push rotary mower, which the grandchildren found fun to use.

**1975**

**2/8 Went to Leachs office & then to his home for mtg & supper. Took Ila Jean to organ lesson. It was cold.**

Congressman Jim Leach states in a letter of recommendation for Myrtle in 1983, "A member of many civic and professional associations such as the Pork Producers and the Farm Bureau, Myrtle has been active in the Republican Party. She has worked in my campaigns since I first sought office and I owe her a tremendous debt of gratitude."

**2/12 Got to Minneapolis at 10 this morn. Ate lunch with them. Went to see stage play Sound of Music this eve. 4-H basketball practice started.**

**3/19 Left this morn for N.P.P.C.** (National Pork Producer's Council) **Congress in KC. Flew. Awful foggy. Went out to eat at Station this eve.**

**5/20 Took Roy over to airport as he had M.B. mtg in Denver. Had Alta, Alma, Velma, Melba & Jeanette here for lunch. 70-80 mile wind came thru.**

**11/7 Left at noon today by plane for K.C. Went to see Red Skeleton show this eve. Ila Jean drove new car to school.**

**12/20 Went to shop for truck and lite fixtures for Xmas. Got Xmas tree home from Whites.**

'Doc' White, the vet, had a Christmas tree farm on the outskirts of Davenport off Brady Street. The tree chosen each year from this field of trees originally sat in the parlor nestled in by the old bay window. After that room was remodeled and the bay window removed, the new spot for the tree was in front of the corner picture window—so the lights would show outside, too. Some of the beautiful long needle pines chosen for that spot were so wide and tipsy they had to be wired to the window frame to hold them upright—especially with the kind of action that occurred around the tree on Christmas Eve!

**1976**

**1/15 Had club here this aft. 100 %.** ( all present) **Went to Pork Banquet this eve & I got bell ringer award & special award from Scott Co. Pork Producers – Surprised!**

**1/18 Bank directors surprised us this eve for our ann.**

**8/23 Went to barbeque in the hills of Idaho this eve. Was quite a thrill. Frank came home for week.** (to be wed to Annette 8/28)

**10/15 Exciting day. Met President at Farmers mtg & had pictures taken with him. Had supper at Annettes & Frank. Went to Leaches birthday dance after we came home.**

Glen, Jean, Roy, President Ford, Myrtle, Ila Jean, Annette and Frank.

**11/2 Carter won over Ford. Leach won over McVinishy. Went to ballisters & then to Leaches house.**

**11/3 Kind of a let down feeling.**

**1977**

**1/16 Roy was on radio this eve for Coop. Went to Elmer Hamans for anniversary supper. It was one of the coldest days ever.**

**2/9 Left for Denver this morn. Rented a car and drove to mountains. Stopped at Central City. Drove the back roads & really got scared.** (narrow mountainside roads) **Stayed at Keystone Lodge.**

**5/25 Went to Chicago with Roy to Meat Board Mtg. Flew up. Nevill butchered a lamb this eve & hung it in our basement.**

**6/9 They are cultivating corn & beans like mad. We need rain badly.**

**9/16 Got my hair fixed this morn. Went to Leaches for tea this aft. Had a party here this eve for winning at Austin.**

Myrtle could really 'make the fur fly' in preparation for company coming! This meant getting out the vacuum hose and sucking up any stray dust balls that may have accumulated. It was especially important to her to get the 'cobwebs out of the corners'. The 'pig table' holding her collection was dusted with extreme care.

**10/21 Had school tour here for 52 people from Dav school. Went to Methodist church bazaar & got things for church supper. They dug potatoes- a lot of them.**

**1978**

**3/21 Had craft class this morn. Mopped kitchen floor this day.**

**3/29 It was 80 degrees this day but still some snow on yard left.**

**5/6 Roy was on panel at Greek Church for "How to Feed the Hungry World". Started in the fields again this aft.**

**7/23 Had 130 people here as Dav. Sister city was here from Germany. (Kaiserlanter) Pork prod. Did chops. Mock wedding too.**

**8/13 Canned some tomatoes & more pickles.**

**1979**

**5/12 Went to Red Rock Dam, bought little baby chicks, ate dinner at church beautiful day. Went to Leaches for supper this eve.**

**9/25 Went to Blackhawk for Breakfast for Leach with Bush. Had school tour here this morn. Glen started to open field for beans. I went to church mtg at Phyllis G.**

**9/29 Butchered 4 of our chickens today. Went to Donna Wesphals wedding & reception this eve.**

**12/23 Made grit vouse today. All went to Scott Co. Park about 4:30 & saw deers. Had cookies and (hot) chocolate in park. Nice day.**

**1980**

**3/30 It was a very rainy ugly day. Stayed home all day. Worked on various things.**

**4/23 Roy planted garden while I hauled anhydrous all day.**
Serving on the coop elevator board, Roy was instrumental in making this sprayed ammonia fertilizer accessible in Eldridge.

**4/27 Ray passed away at 6 o clock this morn.** (cancer) **We were up there till noon. Had birthday dinner at Glens for twins 3rd birthday.**

**5/6 Had lots of kids out for head start. Roy had elevator mtg this eve. I have a bad cold.**

**10/1 Cleaned out the west hall closet today & some shelves in basement. Roy got a call to serve on Agr. Board from Wash. D.C.**

**11/6 Roy flew to Wash D.C. to meet with the 18 men from Agr. Task Force & law office. I went with Jean to Fair Youth banquet at Fairgrounds.**

**12/1 Roy left for Wash D.C. for Reagan Task Force. I took Jean & kids along, too** (to the airport). **Kept the kids overnite as they went to club & party.**

Myrtle and Roy belonged to four social groups originally formed for playing cards (500). "Big Club" (12 members) began meeting monthly right after High School. Little Club had only 8 members, but often had special events including the kids. "Afternoon Club" was the ladies meeting the Third Thursday since 1959—with no babies, but Ila Jean usually slept in the afternoon so she would go along or Roy would help out—and the First Friday group just for their special things such as lunch out once a month. Myrtle noted, "I think it's important to belong to something like that."

**12/24 Frank drove home here at 6:30 Dale at 7:30. Had shrimp, fruedens, jello & bacon**

Frueden ('peace') Recipe: 1pkg yeast dissolved in 1/2 c. hot water, 1 egg beaten, 1T salt, 1 T cardamom, 3 c. milk (scalded) 1/2 c. cream. Pour milk with eggs, beat in 2c. flour, add yeast, mix in 2 1/2 c. more flour, add 1 c. raisins (soaked). Let rise until bubbly (1 hour). Mix again, then fry in oil in round fritter pan.

# Chapter Nine
# "Humble Hall of Fame"

*"Animal collectors rarely care if the item was made yesterday or three hundred years ago. Age is not a factor. As long as the object is in the shape of their favorite animal or has their favorite animal pictured on it, they want it."* Harry L. Rinker from an article about Myrtle's pig collection by Joann Alumbaugh

Myrtle started a special collection of antique pigs in the early 60's. She also was gifted with, and could not resist, any household item in the shape of a pig. Thus, the home became filled with pig this and pig that. The antique and international items were delegated to a large low table in the corner of the old parlor—not to be touched except to be dusted. A pig yard sculpture was kept company by a pig made of farm machinery parts. Others were scattered throughout every room, except the bedrooms upstairs. Roy helped to select and purchase a leather pig footstool that the grandchildren enjoyed 'riding'. It had to be replaced after several years of heavy use..

Roy's actions were driven by his vision of the world beyond the farm and family. Though intent on the immediate, he couldn't help but think in terms of the future.

To walk into their farmhouse is to hear the stories it can tell reverberate from the plaques on the wall to the trophies stacked tightly in the antique dry sink. Excerpts of books, magazines and newspaper clippings about them and their offspring fill bulletin boards, drawers and bookshelves.

Another favorite collection of theirs consists of pictures with several U.S. Presidents, their favorite being George Bush Sr. who announced his candidacy for President on their farm, and visited on other occasions.

## 1981

**1/17 Worked in the house most of day. Man was here this morn as he is writing biography about Quad City men.**

In that book, Roy's involvement in the Reagan Transition Task force is noted. Congressman Jim Leach is quoted, "Half on the list are serious candidates to become the next Secretary of Agriculture. Roy, in many respects, is the sole 'honest broker' among them, in that he doesn't aspire to the position. Ironically, without a question, he would be the finest Secretary of Agriculture of the group; and I am only sorry he made it clear he would like only to help select the next Secretary, not be it." Later in life, Roy wondered what that opportunity would have been like, but notes that he didn't want to go through the scrutiny of the nomination process, with his ninth grade education.

**2/6 Grandma and I went to Chinese place on Div to eat lunch. Roy met with Reagan in Wash. D.C. Dales were home and some of us went to sym to see cellist.**

**4/8 Went to Rural Womens Day this aft. Argentina men were here this aft. Went to Rustic Ridge for pork chop dinner with them for Rotary** (Roy was a charter member of the North Scott Rotary)

## 9/14 Glen showed Grand Champion Truckload. Roy had reserve. 8 out of 10 loads were from Eastern Iowa.

Roy studied in earnest how to crossbreed hogs to make them leaner. When hog fat was no longer needed in great quantities for the war effort—it had been used to grease guns, consumers of pork simply didn't want all that fat on their plate. With friends he made at Oscar Mayer Packing Co. and Iowa State University Extension Services, they found it was in everyone's interest to change the product. Setting aside his fear of failure, he whole-heartedly embarked on a long journey through years of slow changes to reduce the lard on pork by carefully tweaking the breeding of his hogs. His was an example followed by many.

Through diligent record keeping and selection of better breeding stock, the backfat measure gradually decreased measurably. This was something that had not previously been measured. It proved to be a useful and relatively painless measurement to obtain. Earmarking, on the other hand seemed to be a fairly painful way for a baby pig to start the day. By the position of a V shape left by notching along the inverted V shape of the piglet's ear, that pig was marked with a number that would not disappear as the pig grew.

Though it elicited quite a squeal, the piglets were soon playfully twirling around in the fresh straw with their similarly marked littermates. Before long, they would likely cuddle in for comfort beside each other for a quick snack at their mother's udder.

Within weeks, the piglets were weaned from that comfort of mother's milk and offered 'creep feed'. High in protein, this encouraged muscle growth. Roy believed in getting the pigs' feet on the ground (vs. concrete) and usually moved them to a large pen in a field of alfalfa where they could run and play to their hearts content.

Though Roy felt strongly that this outdoor environment kept the pigs strong and healthy, the practice came into practical question as confinement facilities came to be the norm. Still he did not cease to tout its desirability for both the health and growth rate of the hogs.

Vaccinations were also an important part of early swine care. Antibiotics were used only as needed. Vitamins and minerals were the only feed additives used. In competition, which Roy believed to be necessary for improvement, hogs (and cattle) were judged by rate of gain as well as carcass measurements. Animals to be exhibited were identified and sorted out months before. Since there were several major competitions he participated in each year, the process of preparation was ongoing.

The Link included these pictures of Myrtle and Roy's license plate and mailbox in a feature article in 1989

KEPPY'S LICENSE PLATE IDEA WAS FIRST USED IN 1979 WHEN ROY WAS CHAIRMAN OF THE NATIONAL LIVESTOCK AND MEAT BOARD AND SON, DALE, WAS PLANNING HIS PROCESSING PLANT. IT IS STILL IN USE TODAY!

him that he could continue his education only if he wanted to. As none of his older brothers went on to school, Roy decided to get on with farming and raising hogs.

4-H and extension work became

a form of education. A definite advantage of 4-H was meeting other youths at county and state fairs and other educational meetings. In fact, a high point was meeting the girls' county 4-H

president, Myrtle Ec
H dance. Several ye
were married!

Roy and Myrtle st
on their own in 194
farm rented from He

THIS MAILBOX PIG IS MODELED AFTER KEPPY'S CHAMPION BA
AT THE 1962 INTERNATIONAL LIVESTOCK SHOW.

GLENDALE FARM
ROY B. KEPPY

**1982**

**2/1 Roy left at 7 this morn for D.M. & then to Wash. D.C. as he was on state Legislative Comm. Jean and I went shopping for shower gift.**

**2/3 Roy got to visit with Elizabeth Dole. Came home at 3:30 in morn.**

**3/2 Ila Jean brought her bridal dress home & we went to Eddy S. to take pictures.** (preceding her being wed to Dan 3/20) **Dad went to Iowa Producers Bldg Mtg for Scott & Clinton. Moved Irene over to Ridgecrest.** (part of the continuing care village Myrtle and Roy moved to)

**3/7 Mohr group, Greens and Behrens surprised us for breakfast at Ia. Trucking Co. Went to Curran reception at Arsenel Club this aft. Made grit vouse this eve.**

**3/22 Did work in general & cleaned up a little. Took Dumans & went to bring things back to Lucys Cakes & ate at Candlelite. Our barns are full of little pigs.**

**5/5 They are very busy saving moisture & planting corn.**

**6/2 I took 3 pigs to DeWitt to be butchered this morn. I started not to cook for hired help anymore.**

Myrtle had spent many hours cooking so that the men who worked on the farm would 'be fed', but it was becoming more difficult for her to do so. She notes, however, "That (reprieve) only lasted a few days."

**6/22 Chatter box school students were here for school tour. There has been an embezzlement at the bank.**

**7/23 They are busy combining oats here at home. We flew home this morn from N.D. Roy went to Rotary Mtg & I got my hair fixed, worked at market and had 40 yr. class reunion at Jumers.**

Whew, what a day! But this was typical of their schedule for many years.

**7/26 Had 90 some inner city kids this morn & aft thru extension. Alvin Mohr's & us went to Garners corn boil this eve.**

**1983**

**1/3 Roy had appt. at Slack. Made a meat tray for Coop. Glens came home from Atlantic. Grace Dietz was here to start Mother of Year contest.**

**1/8 Got my hair fixed this morn. Brent got old machinery toys out of attic after putting Xmas things away. We all met at Moose & ate supper for all the birthdays.**

**1/13 Roy judge 550 hogs in Denver from 8 to 8. He was really tired. I worked at plant all day. Dale had loin sale. Ate supper with Velma & Ted at Slagels.**

**3/5 Worked at the plant most of the day. After closing Dad mopped everything on hands & knees. Had Glen's kids here this eve. Dales left for Colorado.**

**4/15 Got my hair fixed. Dr. Gingerich, Jim Leach & Glen & Roy had coffee here this morn. Left at noon for Harlan for Merit Mother awards mtg.**

**6/3 Left after Rotary with Grandma & Laurel for Grand Rapids where we met Annettes & stayed over nite. They are looking at houses. We had a picnic along.**

**10/21 Took Grandma to Harlans. Took Laurel to slumber party & Brent & us looked at some trucks. It rained hard all day.**

**12/3 Had wild duck dinner for Frank's birthday. Went to Jane Ewoldts wedding reception & then babysat. All the grandchildren played together today.**

With their differences in age, there was quite a span of years between weddings of the boys and those of the girls. So also, the births of the grandchildren spans about twenty years. Each child was greeted with great joy and enveloped into the family circle. The youngest was always the biggest attraction at family gatherings. Two sets of twins were especially fun. Great Grandchildren add a special touch, too... if only they could touch and be with them more. The worries, weddings and wonders about all these young people gave Roy and Myrtle feelings of purpose and legacy beyond themselves as they aged. It's challenging to remember all of their birthdays, much less where they are when and with whom!

**12/31 Roy helped me get ready for New Years party here. Entertained them with Cabbage Patch doll & chicken song record** (and dance), **about 20 were here. Weather was cold but quiet.**

**1984**

**1/20** Roy left to go to Hilmer Moore ranch in Texas & planes were all fowled up. Shelley & I took Grandma to Riefes.

**3/2** Met girls at ElRancho for lunch & they all gave me a present. Then this eve Dales hosted a big surprise party on me. More presents & even a male dancer. Everyone had fun & lots of laughter.

**4/2** Worked at rural womens brunch this morn. Visited Grandma. Took Laurel to church class, got dried beef from Walcott. Went to Rotary dinner at Westerlins Dorm in R.I. this eve.

**8/2** Was at fair all day. Had butterfly Pork Chops & our picnic. Stayed in S.M.A. Bldg. this aft. Went to Barb Mandrell show this eve.

**8/8** I got a permanent this aft. Helped at corn boil this eve at plant for rotary. Glen found out Sec. Block was coming there next week.

**8/14** Sec. John Block was at Glen's farm. Lunch and all. Nice day. Corn, pork chops, tomatoes were served. Later on went to Jumers for party for Jean Mohr. Orville Sweet & Wayne Walters were here awhile.

**8/20** Just kind of goofed the day away & got things ready for Roy. Had a barbeque at Kent. Horse Farm this eve. Did some shopping.

**9/6** Roy went to Block hearing in Dav. Ila Jean went to Dales for supper.

**10/24 Ila Jean was on radio W.H. O. with overnight casserole recipe. Roy had bank meeting this aft. They picked corn.**

**12/1 Roy was invited over to Sec. Blocks farm with Russians. Brent and Matt went also. Went to Rotary Xmas party at Blackhawk this eve.**

**12/31 Lady from Bett. Library was out to get story on pigs.**

## Pig Collectors Unlimited

### Collecting pigs is favorite pastime of producers, nonproducers

BY JOANN ALUMBAUGH

From planters to pot holders, cookie jars to wind chimes, dishes to jewelry, and endless other possibilities, pig paraphernalia continues to grow in popularity. And there are plenty of people willing to collect it.

There is just something about a pig that endears it to the heart of antique and collectible enthusiasts. But according to collectible expert Harry L. Rinker, other animal collectors feel the same way about their chosen species. Take, for example, members of the American Association of Aardvark Afficionadoes.

"Animal collectors provide the principal exception to my Thirty Year Rule: 'for the first thirty years in anything's life, all its value is speculative,'" notes Rinker.

Myrtle Keppy, Eldridge, Iowa, has been collecting pigs like the here for more than 40 years. Her most treasured pig is th Award" necklace she wears around her neck, given for outst to the pork industry.

**Went to Don Schneckloth. Weather was bad all day & got worse. 9 couples stayed overnite & we had a good time.**

Myrtle remembers, "I had to sleep on the chair because my hip was so bad." The party lasted a little longer than the hosts had anticipated!

**1985**

**1/24 Roy went to Rotary Mtg. this morn. Took some of my pigs to Bettendorf museum for display. Roy & I worked 3 hrs. at plant this eve.**

The 'plant' Myrtle refers to here is Town and Country Meats, a federally inspected packing plant jointly owned by son, Dale and she and Roy. She enjoyed serving customers in the deli when they sold retail meats while Roy served as custodian.

**2/19 Roy chaired the meeting today. We left our Pres. Suite at 2:30. I just stayed in hotel all the time.** (likely writing letters to her girls and catching up on old magazines)

**2/29 Roy was honorary pall bearer at John Schnoor funeral this morn. I visited Grandma awhile this aft.**

**4/1 Went to airport for lunch in new bldg & got Roy home from A.M.I. Mtg in Houston. I didn't lay down all day. Dad came home early for Bank mtg.**

As Myrtle's hip pain continued to worsen, she found it frustratingly necessary to lie down most days.

**8/20 Roy gave up his gavel this afternoon & gave farewell speech this eve at banquet. Had party in our room afterwards. Toured the city today.**

**9/3 Took care of things at bank. Shelled the last corn in the crib. Left at 5 for Sandwich, Ill. Had to drive an extra 14 miles to find a motel. It is hot.**

**9/7 Had sandwiches relishes & tea for about 125 College students for workouts. Worked at plant this aft. Made apple dessert for tomorrow.**

**10/30 Worked in playroom & made Halloween candy. Went to Farm & Fleet to do some Xmas shopping.**

Roy was often called away from the farm leaving Myrtle to 'hold down the fort'. Though their travel in North America was extensive, overseas trips were left to the younger generations.

**Roy.....Myrtle....Dale....Annette......Glen......Ila Jean**

**1986**

**1/21**

**Elaine had club at Moose this noon. The men had Pioneer mtg at moose also. Then he had fair mtg. Then went to see Barb Bush at Library & then to Annas for her birthday.**

**3/30 Easter. Unbelievably warm. 88 degrees. Went to breakfast at 8 church at 9, Easter egg hunt here at 10. Annettes left at 1:30 & then we went to Glens awhile.**

**4/15 Roy went to M.B.**(National Livestock and Meat Board) **Mtg in Chicago for day. I took him over and got him. I went walking with Jeanette K & J. I had appt with Vickstrom. Did some reading.**

**4/22 Roy had bank mtg in D.M. today. Dave Stephens put in his resignation this morn. Was a good day after a lite freeze. I cleaned truck, shopped & raked leaves.**

**5/6 Went to Ladies Republican Luncheon this noon. Glen is finishing planting beans. We sure could use some rain.**

**8/4 Drove to Cedar Rapids & caught plane to Minneapolis & then to Edmonton Canada for Farmhouse Mtg.** (of which Roy was made an Honorary member)

**9/23 Took sheep to Ila Jeans & went to Ames to get Duroc boar. Rained hard most of the day.**

**1987**

**2/14 Cleaned the plant this aft. Glen's 3 were here over nite. Went to Tootsies awhile & then visited Grandma as Anna & group were there to play cards. Started to get little pigs.**

**4/25 Took the kids to have a pony ride. Not Kari tho.** (She was too shy to ride.)**Made cream puffs this eve. Glen started to plant corn.**
**5/16 Helped Charlotte Mohr make dinner for Salvation Army. Took Annie and Grandma to City, Oakdale & Pine Hill cemeteries.**

**6/4 Had lunch with Barbara Bush at Outing Club this noon. Washed windows on inside. Roy cultivated till dark.**

Putting on her everday dress after such an event and doing something common seemed comforting. Roy's need to cultivate (remove weeds from between the crop rows with a piece of equipment pulled behind a tractor) may have served the same purpose for him. Woe to those who do not 'make hay while the sun shines'.

**10/27 Roy had bank mtg this morn. I went to Dittmer's for Barb Bush luncheon. Annette got back from Russia this eve.** (where she had traveled with Deba Leach and other congressional wives for the purpose of peacemaking)

Myrtle and Roy have certainly served as excellent role models in the dedication of time and hard work to a worthy cause.

**Roy and Myrtle with President George Bush Sr.**

When Vice President George H. Bush chose the Keppy farm to announce his candidacy for President, Myrtle had to put up with sniffing dogs in the house for the sake of security. And as he spoke for the cameras in the corncrib, corn fell onto the podium from the bin above. Bush quickly quipped, 'I knew I was in Iowa—the corn state—but I didn't know the corn fell from heaven!'

## 1988

**2/6**
**Took kids and went to Bush rally at Holiday Inn. Took them to their BB practices this aft.**

**2/23 Roy sold hogs $45.50 at 240**(pounds). **Roy got a call to be on a panel in New York.**

**2/29 Sold hogs this morn for $46. I delivered meals for eld.** (elderly) **Meal Site this noon.**

**3/3 Left for Nashville by plane this morn. Annette & Ila Jeans were also there. Went to reception this eve for snacks. We stayed at Opryland. Annette's and Glens at Ramada.**

**3/4 Roy was inducted into the Hall of Fame for Pork at NPPC Mtg at luncheon. Nice affair. Went to barbeque this eve.**

Always with a spirit of pride laced with humility and a sense of tradition, Roy and Myrtle set an example of the responsibilities that come with recognition.

**3/7 Had <u>surprise</u> party for Roy this eve. 2 clubs, Anna & Grandma were out. They brought sandwiches & salads & had** (banana) **splits and cake.**

Preparation for parties would include scooping (or 'dipping up') a large bowl of ice cream from about 2 gallons of a variety of flavors scooped side by side and then refrozen. If everything is cold to start with the ice cream doesn't melt too fast. Strawberries were sugared and hot fudge sauce was made from scratch. Guests would then make their own unique desserts in real glass banana split boats to boot! As Myrtle said, "It makes a pretty centerpiece to start with."

**3/13 Went to Glen's for Pauls birthday dinner today. We got Grandma out. I have a cold. Got some baby rabbits.**

**3/23 Left for N.Y.C. this morn. Staying at Plaza 50. Went to see O Calcutta-nudist. Ate at Marriott. Kind of chilly.**

**3/25 Ate breakfast at Waldorf Astoria. Did some shopping at Macys. Left NYC at 4 this aft. Nice time. Had a much needed rain here at home.**

**5/12 Kept Paul today. Cooked a beef tongue. Grandma is not feeling well.**

**6/1 Left at 9:30 for Ames as Roy had Friends of Ag meeting. I did book work & sewed in Memorial Union. Very dry all over.**

**8/20 Kids played hard together all day. Took them swimming at Bonnies this eve. We met Verlo Butz at Jumers & took them to Happy Joes.**

**11/5 Was a terrible windy cold day. They moved pigs in from the field. Our 7 club ladies went to Mossondon. Roy, boys & Glen went to football game in Ia. City.**

**11/23** Went to our first Grandparent day at Ed White. I gave response from Grandparents. 400 grandparents came. Cleaned house this aft.

## 1989

**3/18** **Glen called Jean from China.** (where he was representing pork producers) **I worked with pictures. Went to Cattlemens supper & dance this eve. Roy took kids to JD** (John Deere) **Day.**

**4/10 Worked upstairs in closet at old cards & things. Went to 4-H basketball games in Eld.**

**5/7 They worked in field today. Glen finished planting corn. Had club at Walt's this eve. I made flower bouquets for Elaine.**

**5/20 Was at Irene E. at 6:30 to help load things on baler trailers for sale which was today & tomorrow. Good day and Good sale. Found out Dorothy E. has another tumor.**

**5/25 Rained a little during the nite. Need it badly. Went to Quad City Downs for Casi** (Center for Active Seniors) **this eve. Roy was kind of lucky.**

**11/2 Roy was a moderater at Swine Genetic Mtg. at Dav. Holiday Inn. Cleaned out the medicine cupboard & did some shopping.**

**12/7 I went to town & did some shopping & watch Chad win at wresling. Went to church ladies Xmas party.**

## 1990

**3/21 Roy went to bank mtg in Eld this morn.Had Dr. appt at Dr Krieter this aft. They took xrays of his knees.**

**4/11 Roy had bank mtg in Dav, this morn, Cooked pork bones for grits so Dale would take some to Annettes for Easter. Helped earnotch pigs.** (She did the holding of the piglets, not the notching of their ears.)

**4/29 Went to CASI style show this aft. Planted trees in wind break place that had died last year.** (in cooperation with the Pheasants Forever movement)

**5/4 Had 3 inches of rain during the night and day. Went to lunch at Jumers with the girls. Roy and I went to see all the water around & ate supper at Grandmas.**

**6/8 I left at 4 this morn with Charlotte M. & Alice D. to breakfast with Bush and Branstad. Came home with Roy & Glen who was at the Mtg. with Pres. Bush. Ate supper with Behrens.**

**7/10 Shelley helped Roy do club calf chores. Roy & I went to sister picnic at Gun Club. I got 1st prize. It rained most of day.**

**9/3 Had club picnic here this noon. Ate in the house. Played cards. Rather warm. Iraq & Kuwait are really in the news. Roy has worked hard on the weeds.**

**9/8 Had 90 boys here for judging workout this morn.** (representing universities from all over the country)

**Almost ran out of ham. Went to campers pig roast at park & then to Jennifer K recap in Walcott.**

'Almost out of ham'—what a catastrophe that would have been! Often using silver award trays, Myrtle always 'fed' visitors. This made for a lot of work, of which she was not afraid. Her generous hospitality has been appreciated by many.

**10/4 Entertained 30 Germans here for lunch. Dale got it started. Betty Clausen delivered chickens this aft.**

**11/15 Had club at Velma A this noon. Helped burn boxes as Dale has so many combos as he is doing them for Saudia Arabay.**

There was a 'burning pile' in the back yard near the garden. Paper, plastics and anything else that would burn was incinerated there. Food garbage went in the 'chicken bucket' kept under the sink. Later, when Roy served as custodian of 'the plant', he burned large quantities of meat boxes. Of course, burning times depended on the wind speed and direction. The fires needed constant attention, which is why it was handy to have the garden nearby so as not to waste time.

**11/22 Herb Plambeck was out here this morn. Bought 2 book from him. Dale, Brent & Jean were here for turkey supper. Glens came later for desserts.**

**12/24 Had our family picture taken at Eds this aft. Had 24 for fruden supper this eve. All family was here. Weather was good but cold**

It looks like they had to schedule a professional family picture to get all of the family in one place at one time!

## 1991

**1/9 Started to clean living room. Went to Durant to get lard. Ate in Walcott. Glen and Roy are figuring farm cost.**

**1/15 Got ready for corn banquet people to come here afterwards. Dipped up ice cream. Started to rain & snow so some didn't come.**

**1/20 Was on cookie co. at church this morn. Then cleaned plant some. Ate in town & came home and ironed big tablecloth.**

Myrtle had an ironing machine called a mangle which looked like it could do just that! Though she became quite adept at using it, like other things, it became difficult to access while stuck in a closet and used to store items on top of it.

**4/1 Boarded the Pres. Boat for her first voyage. Was a perfect day. Glen seeded oats & picked Pheasant Forever corn. No school.**

**5/2 Went in at noon. Got Roy at 2:00. He is sore. Glen finished planting corn. He also has some beans in. <u>Dry</u>.**

**5/24** It rained again last nite so painter didn't come. I made food for Dorothy & took it in. I painted table today.

**5/26** We cleaned out the garage today. Went to Pine Hill Memorial this eve.(where ancestors are buried) Ate at Denny. Hot. Picked 6 quarts strawberries.

**6/15 Helped Annette to clean house for realtor.**(Preparing to sell a house was an unfamiliar experience for Myrtle.) **Ate at 3 this aft & then went to Alysas dance recital. Stayed at Mayflower.**

**7/21** George and Janis & us left for Annettes cottage. We met them at the Ramada & had a picnic of chicken salad.

**8/12** Took boys & Shelley to Scott Co Park this aft. They played on playground.

**9/7** Had 90 kids here for judging team for lunch. Got things ready to go tomorrow. Made juice.

**9/15** We went to Leach brunch then to Eckermann picnic. Cliffords were hostess. Then to Rusty nail.

**1991**

**10/1** Dav. Sister city were here from Germany from 9 to 1. Dale did Am. Cuts. Marion helped me some. Nice day.

**10/11** Roy did not go to Rotary as he thought he was to busy. Went to see boys play at homecoming at N.S.

**11/13 Roy was on the career day program in N.S. Jr. High all day. Went to Play Crafters play this eve.**

**12/4 Roy sold his last 8 hogs today to IBP 40.50 for 266. Got Paul from preschool. I worked on Xmas cards. Roy has a bad cold. Brent was in bad accident in Chicago.** (but OK after complicated surgery)

**1992**

**1/21 Got my hair fixed this morn. Went to Annas for 75 birthday. Went to Outing Club for meeting new Pres. From Osh Gosh, Wisconsin.**

**1/28 Left at 9:30 this morn for Pork Congress. They dissolved the Iowa Porkettes. Went to N.P. Producer banquet. Stayed at Savory.**

This had to have been a disappointment after all the years of work to establish the Porkettes. Yet some women felt it was a positive step as then they were considered to be full members of the Producer organization.

**2/17 Met Ven Horst & she showed me old picture of our house. Did a little shopping. Roy had bank mtg downtown. Roy and I cleaned plant this eve.**

**4/24 Pres. Bush called Dad at 12:50 about N.P.P.C. Export with Russia. He stayed home from Rotary. Cold & nasty.**

**4/29 They started in fields again. Started to plant corn. We went on boat as Roy had bnk mtg this noon.**

**6/8 Went in to visit Dorothy this eve. She is not very well but very very brave.**

**6/21 Dad was at court house most of day for condemnation board.** (Some nearby farmland was 'condemned' for industrial use which was considered by the city to be necessary for economic development.) **I tried to clean house.** (with her sore hip)

**7/6 They tied up club calves today.** (An annual ritual, this was part of 'getting ready for fair') **We worked at plant some. Ate at Harlans this eve.**

**7/20 Delivered Meals on Wheels. Roy had bank mtg this aft downtown. Worked at plant on weeds this eve. Cool.**

**8/2 Roy and Glen left at 6 this morn for Chicago to meet with Pres. Bush on sale to Russia. I brought flowers to church for breakfast for new pastor.**

**8/5 Saw boys give presentation. They go to St. Fair. Stopped by Schreck & found that Roys heart was beating to fast 150.**

**8/8 4-H swine day. Chad got champ pen of 3 & barrow. Took picnic lunch. Went to fair again this eve. I baked apple pie.**

How does one describe The Fair? Though the size and scale of each different fair were remarkably different, the main features and minute details of each were surprisingly similar. Preparation for the 4-H fair, whether county or state, was a big deal. There were not only the animals to think about. Furniture items were selected and refinished, demonstrations written and practiced to perfection, burnt baked goods fed to the cats in favor of a fresh batch and so on. It wasn't possible to just say one day, 'let's go to the fair'—you got ready way in advance—so the anticipation was great! Myrtle often expressed her interest in entering this class or that, because maybe nobody else would. Her motivation was out of concern for the success of the fair—it would fail if exhibits and classes did not have participants. She saw it as a learning opportunity for those who entered exhibits and those who observed.

After entry forms have been mailed, it is time finally to take your entries to the fairgrounds. This is all done on a fairly regimented schedule to avoid congestion.

Nevertheless, it is always a congested mess: people chit chat when they should be moving their vehicles; something is rejected due to lack of proper paperwork; the heat is stifling. This all occurs before the fair actually opens to the public, so exhibitors get a sneak preview while the carnival and food vendors just begin to set up—quite a transformation to see.

Then the fairground gates swing wide and the people pour in! A perfect place for a person to perfect people watching skills, the fair attracts all kinds. Watching young, old and in-betweens pass through the barns while perched on a bale of straw, hours passed in no time at all. Roy was always very careful to keep the barns tidy so as to present a positive image to the consumer. The blare of radios ( it soothes the animals), the smell a mixture of fresh straw, stale manure, oiled hair, sawdust in the show ring and fair food. The fair is to sit on a scratchy bale of hay on a hot day in a barn cooled by the roar of fans and roll a piece of ice flavored by fresh lemon and sugar around on your tongue while being licked by the scratchy tongue of a tame 1000 pound steer! It was easy to become close to those big bundles of beef with their homely, beseeching eyes and their winsome ways...even if they didn't come close to winning the show. By early summer, they wore halters and walked behind a wagon pulled slowly by a tractor. By mid summer they were trained to walk like a dog on a leash. They 'spooked' like horses and would occasionally bolt, possibly to be found nearing the midway or an exhibit building.

The 4-H Building closest to the barns has been named after Roy and Myrtle. They express feelings of humbleness, and are honored to have been remembered this way. It was always important to them that the fairgrounds represent a positive image of agriculture to their city neighbors.

The North Scott Press (Eldridge, Iowa) Wednesday, December 18, 2002 **5A**

**ROY & MYRTLE**

**KEPPY HALL**

This sign was unveiled at the Mississippi Valley Fair board's annual Christmas party Thursday night.                    NSP Photo by Phil Roberts

## 1993

**4/8 Alyssa & Shelley help at rural womens day this morn. Took kids to see movie Huck & Finn this eve.**

**5/25 They still couldn't get to fields. Went to visit Elaine D in hospital. Took Dale & Laurel to Bishops. Kept Paul.**

**6/7 Our Lake is really full. The fullest ever we think. Rained about 6 inces the last few days.**

**8/6 Str.** (steer) **Show day. Had picnic. Neals & Shelly strs got away for them. Went to Rotary corn boil this eve.**

**9/11 Had 80 boys here for judging contest. Left this aft for Ames & stayed in H. Inn**

Donald Olson says in a letter dated 1/21/83, "The Keppy farm has been used over the years as a place to bring 4-H, F.F.A., and college livestock judging teams to work out. Myrtle always assisted in the effort by providing lunch and making the team members feel at home." He goes on to say that, "Judging team members years later will comment on the hospitality of Myrtle." (which indeed they have). "From my standpoint (as Scott County Extension Director) you never had to worry about a crowd at an educational event at the Keppy's. Why? Because you knew you would be well treated."

**9/25 Rained almost all day. Shelley came over & Roy worked on record books. Got groceries this eve.**

**10/7 Roy went to bank loan mtg first & then we got boars from Stan Martens in Postville. Leaves were beautiful.**

**11/26 Went to Laus 50th anniv at Holiday Inn this aft. Were all going to Downers Grove to meet Annettes & then she got sick.**

This was an attempt at a family reunion that unfortunately failed to materialize due to illness. All felt it was a great idea and it was a disappointment that no later attempts were made to reschedule. It is unfortunate that families rarely gather for any length of time after numbers increase and miles separate.

**1994**

**1/5 Kids moved in as G&J are at NPPC mtg in Florida. Got my hair fixed & went to Charlies visitation. Kids all came in too.**

**1/14 Went to George and Janice 50th Ann. Party at Walcott Col. Kind of cold. 22 below. Annette called & said she felt pretty good since Thanksgiving.**

**1/23 Glen's house is all messed up & so they came here for chicken dinner. Glen is in San Diego. Cleaned the plant this aft.**

**3/31 Kids picked up junk in road ditches. Took them to Walcott for supper & then played cards.**

**4/28 Nasty and had a bad dust blowing thing today. They closed 80 for awhile.**

**4/30 Had about 1 inch of snow. Unbelievable! I went on tour to Kalona to quilt show. Went to Tracy & Gene Keppy reception in Walcott.**

**6/1 Glen left for S.F. We had appt with Darland for estate planning.**

Real wealth was measured in their abundance of family and friends. They often commented while looking over the wall of family portraits that "This was our best crop!"

**7/18** (Roy's writing) **Spent day getting ready for tomorrow. Washed rugs on 53rd Street. Ate at Country Kitchen then went to TCBY for treat.**

Following Myrtle's hip replacement surgery, Roy's efforts to keep her diary current were interestingly therapeutic for both he and his hurting wife. He realized how important it was to sustain this lifelong journaling passion.

**7/20** (Roy) **Myrtle has pain today, little wonder. Dr. Roskie said incision 6" long 8" deep (ouch) She can sit up & stand with help.**

**9/12**(Roy wrote) **Got Mom home at 1:30 today.** (her rehospitalization was due to a staph infection that required more surgery) **Lots of activity. 9 grandchildren at times. Nice for them to get together. Had bacon & T** (tomatoes) **for supper. Girls helped a lot, morel & otherwise.**

**10/12 Took Indian corn to HyVee. They wanted more. Picking is going good.**

**10/22 Did different things around the house & started on diaries to get them in order.**

**10/23 Got things back from Sod House. Went to Hickory Garden for Mary & Harolds 45 ann. (Dad adds) Myrtle got all her Diarys in order 1936 to this.**

**11/4** (again Roy) **Much better today. Still pain but attitude better. Lot of company Norma Siever, Janet K, Leon Frick, Jim Leach. Glen Jean and Pail ate here.**

**12/6 Snowed & ice storm came through real fast. Some without lites.**

**1995**

**1/12 Didn't do much.** (Certainly a rare kind of day!)

**1/19 I was to be host for club at Apple River but had to cancel it as bad storm blew in. No school. Had 15 inch of snow.**

**5/29 Memorial Day. No working in field again. The group came here for dinner. Played dominoes new game.**

**6/18 Had Father's Day at Bonnies this morn. Went to Chad & Neals graduation party this eve. Nice party.**

**7/12 Not doing much these days.** (An obvious reference to a period of debilitating pain and its effects on an otherwise industrious woman.) **Oats is not quite ready.**

**7/25 A video was made with Dad about the Meat Board dissolving. Left for Mich at 3 & stayed at New Buffalo, Mich.**

**8/12 Very hot & humid day. Made another gallon of pickles. Elnora & Betty were here awhile this eve.**

**10/18 Scott Campbell took picture of original Pork Board as it is 40 yrs old. We made more corn.**

**12/30 Had our 50th ann. This aft at fairground 1-5. About 900 guests. Nice Day but it snowed later on.**

# Section 4

# Chapter Ten
# "Pay Attention to History"

*"Each generation, in its turn is a link between all that has gone before and all that comes after. That is true genetically, and it is equally true in the transmission of identity. Our parents gave us what they could and we took what we could of it and made it part of ourselves... We, in turn, will offer what we can of ourselves to our children and their offspring."* Fred Rogers

With the opening of the German-American museum in Davenport, Anna and others of the Keppy Family as well as Myrtle's ancestors from the Weise Family, contributed to pulling together the history of the area. Her story here can be a start. When asked what she would like to say to future generations, Myrtle said (10/23/03), "Put more emphasis on history and keep the old treasures!"

## 1996

**1/23 Checked out of Radison & checked in at Blackhawk. These were gifts. Went on boat this aft. Ate at Blackhawk.**

**2/3 Went to Helen Jane for her 75 birthday party this aft & then to Pork Banquet. 40 ann. Glen, Roy & Shelley were on program. Dale got an award.**

**2/26 Roy and I both had appt. at Schreck. Roy had high blood pressure & now we told Kids I had Parkinsons Disease.**

**3/7 Got my hair fixed. Bank had a appreciation nite & they honored Roy as he retired from bank board.**

When asked what she'd like to do during retirement years, Myrtle says "I'd work hard till age 70, then goof off—play cards, go on the boat." Except for restrictions caused by surgery or illness, she's accomplished that. She said she always thought she'd be a housewife when she grew up. Having children definitely added more responsibilities. Asked how she wants to be remembered; "...for being a generous person—does that sound right?"

**3/29** (Roy's writing) **Fri. Got up at 3:45 left for I.C. 4:45 Went to surgery at 7:30 Came back at 5:30 TEN LONG HOURS Went to intensive care at 6:30 Dale was with me today. I stayed overnight.**

**5/7** (Roy) **Glen moved 9 sows & pigs to field today Myrtle is getting stronger but still has pain. She is doing well in P.T. & O.T. Pastor, Clifford, Dale & Carolyn, Annette & Kari (visited)**

**6/2 Hannah was baptized, Todd first communion & boys birthday all in one. Ate brunch at Ila Jeans. church had birthday.**

## Myrtle and Hannah

### 1997

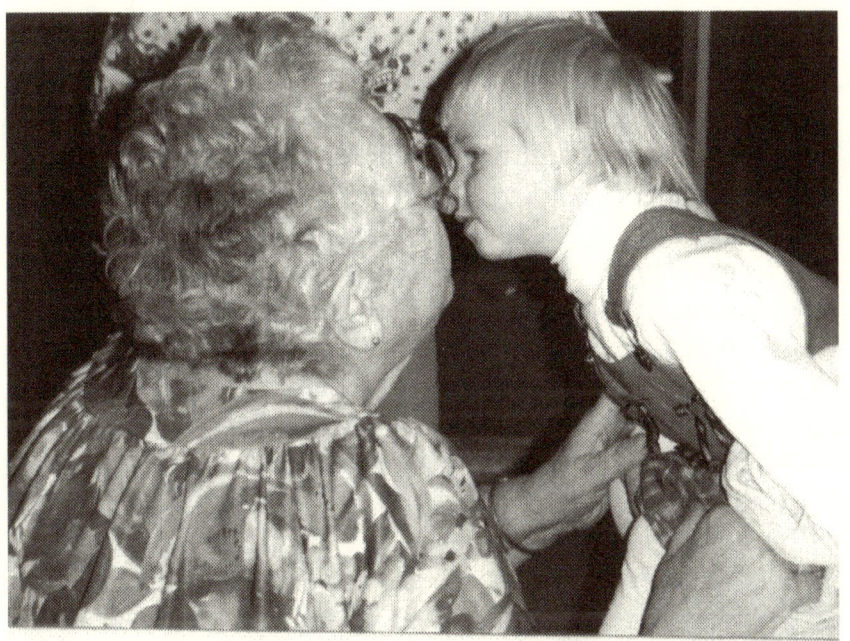

**6/9 The church had a program for 50 yrs of married life. Shelley wore my dress. (wedding) Went to L.G. days.**

**6/20 Elnora was to have club this aft. Instead we went to her funeral. Had lunch at the church.**

**7/4 We were 11 club people for club picnic here this noon. We went to Alvin Mohr afterwards. It was hot & buggy out too.**

**7/9 Went to P.T. this morning. Bad day. Cooled off some and we need rain. They started to put 4-H calves on trailer to lead. Public Iowa T.V. had picture of Keppy farm.**

**7/31 Worked as usual. They are baling straw.**

**8/18 Stayed home all day. Neal left for Ames. Worked on Dads papers for German American book.**

Scrap booking has been important to Myrtle since her 4-H years—long before it became a fashionable hobby. She could not have known then the numerous activities and recognitions received that were to make up her life story, and need to be included in one of many scrapbooks kept carefully through the years. These will be catalogued into the Rural Women's Archives at the University of Iowa Libraries along with her diaries. While reviewing her scrap books with the curator, Myrtle became animated recalling stories about the many special people and important events in her life. Ila Jean was asked to speak at a preservation class about being a 'donor family'.

**9/8 Left for Austin at 11 this morn. Went to picnic at Fairgrounds. They are honoring Roy as he won the most times with individuals, truckloads.** (so much for the rejection of crossbred hogs—first called 'grade' class)

**9/28 Took Anna along & went to October Feast at Jumers. Roys life was on display.**

There may be only a few farm couples who have had the opportunity to 'rub elbows' with as many foreign dignitaries and United States Presidents as have Roy and Myrtle Keppy. When Myrtle tells about the Presidents she has met she sites; Nixon, Johnson-just shook his hand, Ford, Carter and George Bush Sr.-who seemed like a family man. Yet they taught their children (who have subsequently taught their children and so forth) never to be boastful; "Never brag—people don't want to hear it!"

**1997**

**1/7 P.T.** (physical therapy) **this morn. Glens were here supper as boys will be heading back to college Had cherry pancakes & chocolate pudding.**

**3/17 P.T. this morn. Renewed our drivers license. Beings I was using a cane I had to take the driving test. Passed!**

**3/30 Went to sun rise & first service at Annettes church. Had ham dinner at 3. It was snowing this morn. Cold. Kids went swimming at our motel. Easter.** (circled)

**6/6 Went to Village Inn with the girls. I drove myself. Went to get groceries this eve. Started to dig hole for machine shed.**

**6/29 Went to church for repeating marriage vows** (with other couples) **from 50 yrs. Then to Jim Leach lawn party. Then to funeral home & Post Office opening in Eld.**

**7/19 Hot. We did get ¼ inch much needed rain. Went to 5 o'clock church. Ice Cream social at church. Then to John Schroder for pig roast & then to Kent Clausen reception at Eld center.**

**8/6 P.T. this morn. Sorted peaches. They are good. Both of us are using a cane now. Went to fair awhile this eve.**

**8/18** Left at 6 this morn for Branson. Stayed at Welk Hotel. Took us 11 hrs to get there. Saw Welk show this eve.

**9/22** P.T. this morn. Roy took corn over to Elmore Hy Vee. Evryone is getting fever to harvest!

The tension created by machinery malfunction and unpredictable weather at planting and harvest times can indeed manifest itself as sort of an illness.

**10/25** Went to Maysville breakfast. Hair at 9, lunch at Jim Leach, & then to Ned Mohrs birthday. Snow storm out west. Snow storm is coming.

**12/23** Went to P.T this morn. Annette & family came home this eve. We had cherry soup for supper.

**12/24** Bad snowstorm. Brent started from Chicago & got here at 9. Dan started at 1 & got here at seven. It did quit after 6 in. Everyone was here this year-24. Nice Christmas.

**12/25** Took girls & families to Holiday Inn for dinner. Gary and Clifford came this aft. Went to Annas for Xmas this eve. Girls went in early to help. Frank slipped into ditch.

**12/26** Dad & I went to breakfast at Machine Shed. Annettes left about 8:30 p.m. Ila Jean left at 1 p.m. Started to take down Xmas thing. Feel lonesome.

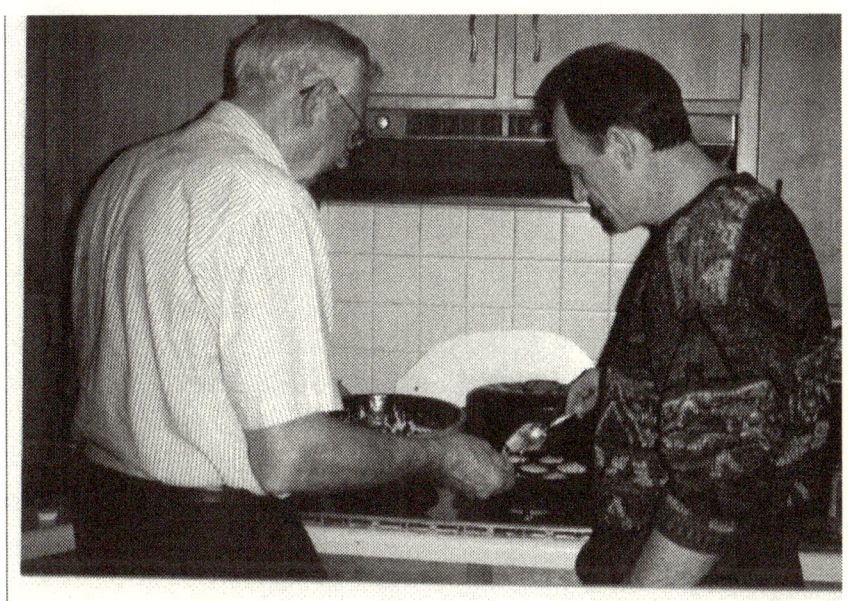

**Roy and Frank frying frueden for Christmas Eve 1997**

# Chapter Eleven
# "Did a Little Bit of Everything"

Myrtle tried to never let anyone leave the house hungry. Though not a problem when friends or relations stopped by—the coffee pot was usually on and there was always a tin of cookies to share—when school tours or judging teams came by the bus or van loads, 'feeding' them was a bit more challenging.

Myrtle would buy loaves of bread, spread them with butter, slap on some ham and serve open face sandwiches with homemade pickles on the side. If she had plenty of advanced notice, pounds of little cocktail wieners were dumped into a large blue roaster and put in a slow oven. When the group arrived, barbeque sauce and grape jelly were slathered on the tasty treats.

What did they come to see? Animals, crops in the fields, and the farm place itself. But mostly, it was the connection with an honest-to-goodness farmer. Myrtle had it right—let them leave with a good taste in their mouths. It is likely those visitors didn't soon forget their experience at the Keppy farm. College students who came as judging teams also learned about pork promotion. Foreign farmers and diplomats found hospitality in the midst of strangers. And politicians went away with more than they bargained for—pork under their belts!

Some of the inner city youth arrived and left holding their noses, but there is no doubt that they had their eyes opened as they heard about farming and took a taste of its outcome. Having experienced the farm with all of their senses (minus possibly olfactory) they will not easily have forgotten it—probably their first and last such experience. A week or so after a school tour, Roy and Myrtle would usually receive a packet in the mail full of thank you notes and crayon drawings from the impressionable students. Special pictures and notes have been kept through the years.

An autograph/guest book was also kept recording foreign visitors, who often noted how meaningful and memorable their visit had been. During those visits, everything else came to a halt in order to attend to the visitors. At other times, however, Myrtle and Roy were intent on doing 'a little bit of everything'!

## 1998

**1/3 Did a little bit of everything.**

**2/8 Stayed home all day. Was a cold nasty day. Made out Valentine cards for all of the Grand Children.**

**2/14 Went to Old Country Buffet for noon for Ann guests. Went to 4-H Co. banquet this eve.**

**2/15 Went to Walcott to hear Anna give a history about Keppys. Roy had to get her & 2 other people. Did some baking.**

**2/21 Spent all day at Tournament where Kari played. Fun. Just ate what we had brought. In room. They gave us a birthday party & Beanie Babies.**

**7/6 Went to Lancer grill for reunion of Triple A office gals. Rained again.**

**7/22 Glen has got a little field left to do beans. Rained last nite. Dad went to Rotary & I went to Merit Mother luncheon at Bishops.**

**9/1 Made another batch of tomato juice. My left leg really bothers me. Nice weather out.**

**9/19 We are doing a lot of bundles (corn) did 150 today**

**9/26 Ila Jean & N & H left for home at 10 this morn. All 3 kids are home from college. Fed everyone this noon – liver.**

**11/9 We didn't go to Sportsmans dinner as I was in hospital. Only walked a little. Roy is coming here most of the time.**

During these long days of hospitalization, it may have helped Myrtle to remember some of the many accolades received through the years. One in which she took great pride was the Iowa Merit Mother Award in 1983—through which she enjoyed new friendships. After many years of 'making it a point' to visit others who were hospitalized, when she felt well enough she enjoyed the visits of countless friends, neighbors and relatives.

**1999**

**1/2** (Roy is writing) **Sat. Dr. Melleia came in, wants xray tomorrow. Snowed all day, wind out of N.E. blowing and drifting. I staid over again tonight. We watched foot ball & played some cards. Tonight Lawrence Welk entertained.**

**2/10** (Roy) **Today Myrtle started to put more wt on her left leg. It went really well (nock on wood) Velma Spies, Philes G & Clifford. Iowa beat Minn.**

**3/1 Glens brought supper over this eve. Got my hair fixed by Jackie S. who came out. My 75 yrs old birthday.**

**3/19 We went to Dr. Sobeth - she is a top Dr. for Parkinson & she said I did not have Parkinson & took all medicine away. Dad was on panel for farmers at Rotary. Went to Glens for supper so Paul could give his tractor talk.**

**3/27 Made dinner for Gary, Glen & Paul. I'm not doing good at all. Listened to Guy Lombardo this eve.**

**3/28 Went to Godfather Pizza to see about Pork Producers are promoting Pork. I fell on my back in living room. I am back on Park. Medicine.**

**5/26 They are busy making good hay. Roy is driving tractor.**

**6/24 We have 11 little kitten up by the door. The Mothers brought them out. Went to Rotary party in the new conference room by Lady Luck.**

Forever on the lookout for baby animals, Myrtle was often called upon to help save little lives. In a letter to a daughter she notes, "We are getting little pigs now so you know the extra work. This noon I got one going in the house. He was in a corner and was cold." This is only one of many baby pigs, lambs, chicks and ducklings that took their turn at being warmed, and consequently saved, on the open oven door in Myrtle's kitchen. Her occasional brisk rubbing of the small creature brought back life when the animal had nearly succumbed to the elements.

**6/29 Decided where we were going to give our CT Stock to. Had appt at Jack & then sent forms to Grandchildren. Froze some R. Rasberries.**

**7/31 Jackie fixed my hair. Went to Bix this morn. Dales wedding at 4 this aft & then reception at Villa. Nice crowd & good food. Got our telephone stock money. Weather is much cooler.**

**2000**

**1/1 Millium year. Everything is hooked to this word. Went to...** (entry left unfinished)

**1/5 P.T. this morn. Pat & Dee cleaned here today & we didn't know they were coming.**
The 'luxury' of having someone else clean the house was a Christmas gift that was a big help to them, but hereafter prompted them to clean-up before the cleaning ladies came.

**1/12 Went to Red Crow for lunch with Laura Bush. Mild Winter. Got Annette from bus station from G.R.**

**5/29 Had picnic here at home. Kardels, Paustian,Bernick, Janet for ham dinner. We ate in our kitchen & then played 6 rounds of 500**

**5/30 We were all in** (tired out) **after yesterdays club here.**

**9/13 Guess what? We had another storm go thru here early morn & our lites & everything went off. Didn't go on until in the afternoon.**

The 'playroom' was actually used for play by the kids and grandkids, but it also contained a myriad of stuff that didn't seem to belong anywhere. For a time, it was where the typewriter stayed to be used. The old Singer sewing machine maintained its permanent spot in the corner. Possibly the memory of Myrtle's run in with that needle sewing right through her thumb made her less inclined to spend more time in that room, even to clean it.

**10/26 Started to think more about cleaning the playroom.**

**11/17 P.T. this morn. Roy went to Rotary. Against Roys wishes I started to clean playroom.**

**11/22 Got working in playroom & almost done. We cleaned a corner at a time**

One of Myrtle's favorite diary entries was 'Did a little bit of everything.' Only she could be sure exactly what that actually meant, but it captures the sense of experiencing a little bit of a lot. Computers store tiny 'bits' of data that when used together can produce fantastic results. Five-year-diaries come in small bits of information, yet when taken together, over many years, they capture a life story!

## Roy and Myrtle 1999

**"Taken after they gave us a plaque for doing things for the fair. There were five of us."**

# Epilogue

*"More than any other source, a regularly kept diary offers a sense of pace and rhythm of family life"* (Lichtman)

Exploring human beings' daily lives through diary entries could be considered voyeurism. Yet, an 'authorized biography' such as this releases one from guilt for having been observer and reporter. The difficulty lies in the interpretation of the written word. Even personal interviews of participants tend to revise the past according to present values. But as Ker Conway notes, "...that magical opportunity of entering another life is what really sets us thinking about our own." Though sometimes somewhat confused by Parkinson's disease dementia, Myrtle enjoyed 'reliving' the days of her life through her diaries. Roy, at age 80 and weakened by leukemia, had trouble sticking with it to make comments, but seemed to enjoy seeing their lives unfold in print. Both were often able to provide clarification, perspective and insight during the compilation of this biography.

Many authors have worked at capturing the past recently. Daniel notes, "... time has brought us to a point where young people have a great hunger for discovering enduring values..." and that "loss of continuity in the generations of our families is a tragic flaw in our society." There is much to be learned from our ancestors. As shared by Maxwell,

*"We are living in days of change;*

*My grandfather had a farm.*
*My father had a garden.*
*But I've got a can opener."*

Though some of the branches of the family tree remain connected to the farm, the farming is now very different. There was some consideration of preservation of the farmplace, yet it remains available for commercial development. Hopefully, the words of this biography will help to preserve the life of the farm as it was from the time Roy and Myrtle first moved there to the end of the century. The sharing of this story is a continuation of their generous gifts to generations of the future.

After moving to an assisted living apartment, Myrtle graduated to a motorized wheel chair while Roy put his Lazy Boy chair to good use. Their concern for and attention to their many friends and large, growing family continued. Both celebrated eighty years of life. Family and friends appreciated their wisdom and longevity ... their presence being their present to all.

Paraphrasing from the Bible in 1 Corinthians 15:3, "What I received I passed on to you as of first importance". Preparation of this biography has taken a good portion of three years. Reading of the diaries and sorting highlights and examples of daily life was a painstakingly loving task. It was prayerfully undertaken on behalf of future generations in honor of the past.

Myrtle and Roy would agree "There are a lot of ways to become a failure, but never taking a chance is the most successful."(Maxwell) This effort in sharing the past with future generations has been the chance of a lifetime. Though plagued by major 'gaposis, and occasional inadvertent inaccuracies, just attempting to compile and summarize this information has been a prayerful effort to capture the essence of two very special people. Thank God for such people—the wind beneath our wings!

# Appendix

# Presidents of the later part of the Twentieth Century

Franklin Roosevelt (1933-1945)

Harry Truman (1945-1953)

Dwight Eisenhower (1953-1961)

John Kennedy (1961-1963)

Lyndon Johnson (1963-1969)

Richard Nixon (1969-1974)

Gerald Ford (1974-1977)

Jimmy Carter (1977-1981)

Ronald Reagan (1981-1989)

George Bush (1989-1993)

Bill Clinton (1993-2001)

George W. Bush (2001- )

# List of Pictures/ Recipes

# People in the Story

Myrtle

Roy

Some Relatives—
Mildred and Valentine
Laura and Peter Wiese
Bertha an d Jochim ('Gumpa and Gumma')
Clifford/Dorothy: Gary/Patti (Kayla, Sarah and Kyle)

Henry and Anna

Anna

Henry/Norma

Charlie/Elnora

Ray/Jeanette

Carolyn/Dale

Children, grandchildren and great-grandchildren—

Glen/Jean: Chad, Neal/ Erica, Shelley/Chuck
(Alayna), Paul

Dale/: Brent/Beth (Baylee, Ethan), Laurel/Mark
(Archie)
Tamia: Kyle, Casey

Annette/Frank: Alysa, Kari, Kyle

Ila Jean/ Dan: Todd, Noah, Hannah

Lifetime friends—

George/Janice

Walt/Elaine ("She was my best friend.")

# Bibliography

Baraks, Gloria et.al, *Profiles in Leadership, Dynamic Men and Women of the Quad Cities,* Quest Publishing Rock Island, IL 1981.

Daniel, Lois *How to Write Your Own Life Story,* Chicago Review Press 1980.

Direct Link, Peoria, IL Spring/summer 1989.

Eckermann, Myrtle 'Diaries", January 1938-January 1946, LeClaire Township, Scott County, Iowa.

Fulford, D.G. *One Memory at a Time* Doubleday NY 2000.

Gibbs, Terri, Ed, *Reflections from a Mother's Heart* Word Publishing, Dallas, TX 1995.

Greene, Bob and D.G. Fulford *To Our Children's Children* Doubleday NY 1993.

Keppy, Myrtle "Diaries", January 1946- Dec 2000, Sheridan Township, Scott County, Iowa.

Keppy, Myrtle and Roy, personal interviews 2003, Davenport, Iowa

KerConway, Jill *When Memory Speaks* Knopf, NY 1998.

Lichtman, Allan J. *Your Family History* Vintage Books, NY 1978.

Maxwell, John It's *Just a Thought...But It Could Change Your Life* Honor Books, OK 1996.

Polking, Kirk *Writing Family Histories and Memoirs* Betterway Books, Cincinnati, OH
*1995*

*Quad City Times* Davenport, Iowa

Rogers, JoAnne Ed. *The World According to Mister Rogers,* Hyperion Books 2003.

Sturdevant, Katherine Scott Organizing *and Preserving Your Heirloom Documents* Betterway Books, Cincinnati, OH 2002

The North Scott Press, Eldridge IA (various dates)

# About the Author

Annette Remsburg felt her childhood years encompassed the best of both worlds—farm living near a city. Farm life provided her with a multitude of memorable experiences: birth of animals, constant care of them and their varied deaths. She learned the value of hard work and long hours amidst a loving family.

A wife and mother, Annette has always made time to read, study and write. She graduated from Iowa State and Michigan State Universities and completed the Writing Course through the Institute of Children's Literature. An enthusiastic reader herself, she currently tutors dyslexic students. Her hobbies as a resident of Michigan include gardening and kayaking. Journaling is part of her journey through life as well.